Welcome to Church Music and The Hymnal 1982

T0275378

Welcome to Church Music and The Hymnal 1982

Matthew Hoch

Morehouse Publishing
NEW YORK

Morehouse Publishing
19 East 34th Street, New York, NY 10016

Morehouse Publishing is an imprint of
Church Publishing Incorporated.
www.churchpublishing.org

Cover design by Laurie Klein Westhafer
Typeset by Vicki K. Black

Library of Congress Cataloging-in-Publication Data
Hoch, Matthew, 1975– author.
    Welcome to church music and the Hymnal 1982 / Matthew Hoch.
        pages   cm
    Includes bibliographical references.
    ISBN 978-0-8192-2942-7 (pbk.) -- ISBN 978-0-8192-2943-4
    (ebook) 1. Episcopal Church--Hymns--History and criticism.
    2. Hymnal 1982. I. Title.
    ML3166.H63 2015
    264'.03023--dc23
                                          2014034813

Printed in the United States of America

To Trinity Church in Boston, Massachusetts,
where I fell in love with the music of the Episcopal Church
and met and married Theresa,
the love of my life and mother of our three children;

to St. Peter's Episcopal Church in Rome, Georgia,
where I cut my teeth as an Episcopal choirmaster; and

to Holy Trinity Episcopal Church in Auburn, Alabama,
where I hope to spend the remainder of my days.

Contents

Acknowledgments

Writing a book is always a group effort, and I am grateful to several individuals for their support throughout this project. Nancy Bryan, editorial director of Church Publishing, was enthusiastic about this book from the beginning, and I would like to thank her for guiding me through the proposal and writing process. Her wisdom was invaluable in shaping the manuscript, and it would have been a very different book without her insights. Production manager Ryan Masteller efficiently shepherded me through the production phase, patiently answering my many questions and welcoming my thoughts throughout the process. The expertise of copyeditor and typesetter Vicki Black also greatly improved the final product, and I am grateful for her meticulous work. I am also immensely thankful to Carl P. Daw, Jr., who graciously proofread the entire manuscript during the final editing stages.

Several mentors from my past were also pivotal to my training as a church musician, as I would like specifically to thank Roger Ard, Richard Coffey, George Damp, Brian Jones, Donald Nally, and Helmuth Rilling for teaching me so much about liturgy and music.

Perhaps most important, I am indebted to my wife, Theresa. Completing this manuscript was all-consuming, and I could not have written this book without her patience and support.

Prelude

Easter morning on Copley Square in Boston is cool and bright. The sun streams through the LaFarge stained glass windows as two thousand parishioners make their pilgrimage into the nave of Trinity Church carrying bells of various assortments— some brought from home and others, smaller, distributed by the ushers. After the organ prelude, a brass fanfare signals the beginning of the opening hymn—"Jesus Christ Is Risen Today"—sung full-throated by the congregation as the choir and clergy process in festal pageantry. A thousand bells ring with every utterance of "Alleluia." The euphoria climaxes on the fourth and final stanza, now played and sung a tad slower and a step higher with an alternate organ harmonization and an ethereal treble descant, perfectly depicting the risen Christ in a blaze of aural splendor....

Easter morning during my years at Trinity Church Boston remains one of my most profound spiritual experiences, yet I could have just as easily cited half a dozen others: a quiet candlelight Lessons and Carols service on a snowy Christmas Eve in a small city in Connecticut, a chilly autumn evensong in New York City, and a meaningful performance of *Olivet to Calvary* on a warm Palm Sunday afternoon in a college town in the Deep South were also transformative experiences for me. Every faithful churchgoer will inevitably have his or her own cherished memories of worship, reflecting experiences as diverse as the people, regions, and parishes themselves. A paperless service in a small church in Montana, a Taizé service in California, or a jazz-influenced "coffee-house" in Michigan are a few examples of the many ways in which music and worship are inexorably linked. For me—and I suspect for many others—music is an integral part of worship. The intellectual, emotional, spiritual, and musical elements are so entwined with each other that I often cannot tell where one component starts and another begins. The most significant spiritual experiences of my life have been complemented by the sounds of sacred music.

Music unquestionably heightens emotional experiences. Can one imagine watching an epic film without its soundtrack? Spiritual experiences are similar: the music enhances the liturgical drama of a particular moment in the service or season. The worshipper is moved by what he or she hears, and—consequently—feels. Oliver Sacks, in his bestselling book *Musicophilia: Tales of Music and the Brain,* notes that

> We humans are a musical species no less than a linguistic one. This takes many different forms. All of us (with very few exceptions) can perceive music, perceive tones, timbre, pitch intervals, melodic contours, harmony, and (perhaps most elementally) rhythm. We integrate all of these and "construct" music in our minds using many different parts of the brain. And to this largely unconscious structural appreciation of music is added an often intense and profound emotional reaction to music. "The inexpressible depth of music," Schopenhauer wrote, "so easy to understand and yet so inexplicable, is due to the fact that it reproduces all the emotions of our innermost being, but entirely without reality and remote from its pain. . . . Music expresses only the quintessence of life and of its events, never these themselves."[1]

Many of us have experienced this very phenomenon during worship: that moment when the music perfectly matches the text and raises it to a new level where words cannot go by themselves. The perfect marriage of tune and text evokes a profound emotional/neurological experience. Textless—or "absolute"—music can transport us to spiritual places as well, as when an organ prelude or improvisation perfectly complements the season or liturgical action. And perhaps nothing is more fulfilling than singing together, making music as a spiritual community. Although difficult to articulate in words, music has profound theological and spiritual content for many people.

This book—part of the Morehouse "Welcome to" series—is devoted to church music with particular emphasis on the musical liturgy of the Episcopal Church and its official hymnal, *The Hymnal 1982*. It is intended to be a vehicle for parishioners to explore the history, structure, and meaning of liturgical music, its synergy with the Book of Common Prayer, and its role in making worship more meaningful. It must be emphasized that this book is an introduction—nothing more, nothing less. It is my hope that parishioners hungry for more knowledge about the music of the Episcopal Church will continue their journey by exploring the resources listed in the bibliography.

The music of the Episcopal Church is one of its richest traditions. I was not born into an Episcopal family, but became a devoted Episcopalian soon after I fell in love with the music. For me—and I suspect for many others—it was the worship experience for which I had waited my entire life. By writing this book, I hope to welcome many others to the Episcopal Church by introducing them to its magnificent music.

NOTE TO THE READER

Throughout this book, readers are frequently encouraged to look up references in both *The Hymnal 1982* and the 1979 Book of Common Prayer. Page and hymn numbers will be provided to these texts, so readers should have both volumes at hand. The one-volume edition of the combined prayer book–hymnal, available from Church Publishing, is a fine resource as well.

Readers will also notice a number of abbreviations and perhaps unfamiliar text styles in this book. The 1979 Book of Common Prayer will often be referred to as "BCP," for example, and hymn tunes will appear in capital letters. In *The Hymnal 1982*, the name of the hymn tune is listed in italics (*Hyfrydol, Easter Hymn*), but all-capital letters are another system that is frequently used to indicate tune names (HYFRYDOL, EASTER HYMN). Capital letters are used in this book to eliminate confusion between other italicized titles, such as book titles, major works, and terminology from foreign languages.

A Brief History of Music in the Episcopal Church

Hallelujah!
Praise God in his holy temple; *
    praise him in the firmament of his power.
Praise him for his mighty acts; *
    praise him for his excellent greatness.
Praise him with the blast of the ram's-horn; *
    praise him with lyre and harp.
Praise him with resounding cymbals; *
    praise him with loud-clanging cymbals.
Let everything that has breath *
    praise the Lord.
Hallelujah!

Psalm 150 (BCP 807–808)

Music and worship have always been inextricably linked. Psalm 150, above, makes clear that active music-making has a part of worship since ancient times. The psalms themselves were hymns of praise that were intended to be sung, and the Bible contains many other references to singing as a mode of worship. For many Christians, the presence of music and the

1

act of singing or listening heightens worship. This chapter briefly outlines the history of music in the Episcopal Church and its "parent," the Church of England, and discusses some of the qualities and traditions that make Episcopal church music unique.

While music is an integral part of worship in any religion or denomination, this book is primarily concerned with the music of the Episcopal Church. The Episcopal Church—a member of the worldwide Anglican Communion—has its roots in the Church of England. We start with a brief history of Episcopal church music against the backdrop of the Church of England in the sixteenth century, when it separated from the Roman Catholic Church with the Act of Supremacy in 1534, followed by the Act of Uniformity and the publication of the first English Prayer Book in 1549.

MUSIC AND THE REFORMATION (1485–1549)

The period from 1485 to 1603 was known as the Tudor period in England and Wales, signifying the rule of the Tudor dynasty. Fifteenth-century England was Catholic, and the music composed for churches primarily consisted of polyphonic settings in Latin. (Polyphony is one of three primary textures in music, meaning that music consists of more than one melodic line.) Around this same time, choir schools were established in England. These were institutions where boys received intensive musical training as singers and musicians. At a young age, they were groomed to lead worship in parishes and cathedrals. Although a distinctly Anglican form of worship had yet to emerge from the Catholic Church, the establishment of these English choir schools laid a foundation for Anglican music that would persist over the next four hundred years. Similarly, the liturgical calendar of the Catholic Church—complete with its distinct seasons and feast days— had a significant influence on the worship and music of the Church of England that emerged during the sixteenth century.

In 1534, Henry VIII broke away from the Catholic Church via the Act of Supremacy. As Henry's reasons for desiring independence from Rome had less to do with theology than with securing an heir to the throne, the liturgy of the early English Church—and its music—remained close to that of the Catholic Church during his reign. Henry did appoint Thomas Cranmer as Archbishop of Canterbury in 1533, however, and under Cranmer's supervision several important innovations were implemented, including the publication of William Tyndale and Miles Coverdale's "Great Bible" in 1539, which was ordered to be placed in all churches so that by 1543 all readings were to be delivered in English instead of Latin. Coverdale's superb translation of the Psalms is still in use in many Anglican churches today. Archbishop Cranmer was also responsible for the development of the first Book of Common Prayer, published in 1549.

THE ESTABLISHMENT OF AN ANGLICAN MUSICAL TRADITION: 1549–1644

The Act of Uniformity in 1549 imposed a uniform service book in English: The Book of Common Prayer. This establishment of an English prayer book is perhaps the most significant event in the history of Anglican church music. For the first time in England's history, a new liturgy existed that was entirely in the vernacular. The 1549 prayer book went through revisions in 1552 and 1559, each revision more radical than the next. The final revision of the Book of Common Prayer occurred in 1662, and this version remains the official Book of Common Prayer for the Church of England.

Some of the liturgical changes introduced by the Book of Common Prayer and its revisions significantly affected the music of the church. Two offices—Matins (Morning Prayer) and Evensong (Evening Prayer)—replaced the eight offices of the monastic tradition. The Book of Common Prayer also offered new translations of texts, including graduals, alleluias, tracts, sequences, antiphons, and responsories. As a result, most of the music that had been sung in worship up until this point was rendered obsolete virtually overnight. The word "Communion" replaced "Mass," and the *Kyrie* was replaced with a recitation of the Decalogue (the Ten Commandments) during the Eucharist.

A new ordinance also required that the entire Psalter be sung at Morning Prayer and Evening Prayer over the course of each month. The psalms were organized into sixty distinct parts: thirty groupings of psalms for Morning Prayer and the other thirty for Evening Prayer. The 1979 edition of the Book of Common Prayer still reflects that organization of the Psalter. The emphasis placed on psalmody is one of the distinctive features of Anglican worship, and the singing of psalms (often to Anglican chant) remains one of the Episcopal Church's most loved traditions.

In 1554, Queen Mary I—the only surviving child of Henry VIII and Catherine of Aragon—attempted to restore Catholicism to England. Although her executions of Protestants earned her the notorious nickname "Bloody Mary," her "restoration" was short-lived, and following her death in 1558 her younger (and Protestant) sister Elizabeth I ascended to the throne. Elizabeth cautiously returned to the reformed tradition through a series of calculated compromises that historians refer to as the Elizabethan Settlement. Over the course of her long reign, most of the country became loyal supporters of the Church of England.

Elizabeth also was the first monarch of the Reformation to weigh in on matters pertaining to music. In her Injunctions of 1559 she ordered that in worship

> there be a modest distinct song, so used in all parts of the common prayers in the church, that the same may be as plainly understood, as if it were read without singing, and yet nevertheless, for the comforting of such that delight in music, it may be permitted that in the beginning, or in the end of common prayers, either at morning or evening, there

> may be sung an hymn, or such like song, to the praise of Almighty God, in the best sort of melody and music that may be conveniently devised, having respect that the sentence of the hymn may be understood and perceived.

During Elizabeth's long reign she favored and encouraged complexity, elaboration, and high ceremony in church music.

Upon her death in 1603, Elizabeth was succeeded by King James I. Although James did not issue any decrees that directly influenced church music, his greatest impact on the liturgy was undoubtedly his sponsorship of a new translation of the Bible, which was published in 1611 as the Authorized Version. The King James Bible quickly established itself and remains the most ubiquitous English translation of the Bible. James also continued to support the innovations and creativity of the Elizabethan era. By the time of his death in 1625, the Church of England—and its music—was well established.

This prosperous era also saw the invention of the anthem, a choral setting in English of a biblical or religious text. This genre would inspire composers over the course of the next 450 years, leaving a rich body of distinctly Anglican choral music.

THE INTERREGNUM, RESTORATION, AND GEORGIAN ERA: 1644–1830

In 1644, two years into the English Civil War, the Long Parliament abolished the Book of Common Prayer. This led to an interim period during which a Presbyterian form of worship was espoused. Churches were ransacked, stained glass windows and organs were destroyed, and choral services ceased. Like Catholics, Anglicans became a persecuted sect worshiping in secret. King Charles I was executed in 1649, which led to a period of eleven years with no monarch. This stretch of time came to be known as the Interregnum, literally meaning "between kings," and very few compositions survive from this bleak era, which fortunately was short lived. The Church of England with its Book of Common Prayer was restored as the established church when Charles II took the throne in 1660. The 1662 Act of Uniformity introduced a final revision of the prayer book; this version is still used by the Church of England today.

The complexities of the Elizabethan and Jacobean eras gave way to a simpler style of English church music in Restoration England. Choral music was generally written in fewer parts, and the "short service" reduced the canticles for Morning Prayer and Evening Prayer to two for each service: the *Te Deum* and *Jubilate* for the former and the *Magnificat* and *Nunc dimittis* for the latter. This short service format is still in use today. The anthem continued to evolve, and instruments—a signature innovation of the baroque era—found their way into the churches, with anthems sometimes including a complement of strings or brass fanfares.

The period of English history known as the Georgian era takes its name from the successive reign of four monarchs, all of whom were named George. At the beginning of this era, George Frideric Handel was the greatest living composer in England. Handel never held a church position, focusing instead on writing Italian operas and English oratorios. Nevertheless, his style influenced the church music of the Georgian era, and choirmasters appropriated some of his oratorio excerpts for use in liturgical worship. During the second half of the century, Joseph Haydn and Wolfgang Amadeus Mozart were at their creative pinnacle, and this distinctly Viennese style influenced Anglican composers as well. Perhaps the greatest contribution of the Georgian era was the establishment of Anglican chant as the primary vehicle for psalm recitation.

CATHEDRAL VERSUS PAROCHIAL TRADITIONS
Although cathedrals were the epicenter of the evolution of Anglican church music, smaller parishes located in rural areas of England were developing their own independent traditions. These two distinct traditions were maintained until the nineteenth century, when a more unified style emerged. Before

proceeding into a discussion of this "golden era" of the mid-nineteenth century, it is worth taking a moment to explore the differences between cathedral and parochial traditions.

Cathedrals

Cathedrals, with their elaborate architecture, magnificent organs, and large choral forces, were the venues that boasted perhaps the greatest productivity and innovations in Anglican church music. The word "cathedral"—from the Latin *cathedra* or "seat"—simply refers to a church where the bishop is seated, and therefore the principal house of worship within a designated region (called a diocese). It does not necessarily imply a large church or music program, but more often than not, cathedrals are considerably larger in scope and scale than most parishes.

In large cathedrals, the choirs were well-trained and could easily execute difficult pieces of choral music. Composers took advantage of the split chancel area to write many pieces for double choir as well. The abilities of these choirs established that very little congregational singing took place; the choir and organist did most of the music-making. It was the smaller parishes without the advantage of choirs and organs that established a congregational singing tradition in the Anglican Church.

Parishes

While many Episcopalians feel strongly that their congregations should have opportunities to participate in music-making, the tradition of congregational singing was actually born out of necessity—the lack of trained choirs, quality organs, and organists—more than any theological perspective. Congregational singing in the Anglican Church was borrowed from the Lutherans and Calvinists, who engaged in congregational hymn-singing from their inception. Metrical psalms sung by the congregation began to be preferred to Anglican chant formulas. Over the course of the seventeenth and eighteenth centuries, a musical culture emerged in smaller parishes starkly different from what was taking place in the cathedrals.

In the early nineteenth century, the Oxford Movement brought some of the cathedral traditions into the smaller parishes, including accessible anthems and psalmody. The men and boys in the choir began to wear surplices, as they would in cathedrals or colleges. Cathedrals absorbed some of the parochial traditions as well, especially the use of congregational hymns. Thus the boundary between these two began to blur, and over the course of the nineteenth century a more unified tradition was established.

A Unified Tradition and a Golden Era: 1830–1922

The end of the Georgian era coincided with the Oxford Movement, during which high church Anglicans who desired a reinstatement of lost ancient Christian traditions sought to return to worship traditions from the early and medieval church that were in some ways more "Catholic." It also began an era when large cathedrals and small parishes began to adopt each other's traditions. More elaborate liturgical traditions found their way into small parishes, and congregational hymns began to be introduced in cathedrals. Interestingly, while a unified tradition emerged, the style of English church music itself continued to move forward, almost completely unaffected by the Oxford Movement. Over the next forty years, English church music flourished as it never had before in its history. In 1872, John Stainer was appointed as organist at St. Paul's Cathedral in London, and his program set a new standard for excellence.

During this era, the first colleges devoted to training church musicians were also established. Frederick Ouseley founded St. Michael's in Tenbury in 1856, and Trinity College in London was founded in 1872 for the purpose of training church musicians. The publishing industry also began to produce a large body of sacred music. Most of their collections consisted of accessible anthems that could be performed with success at small parishes. Although most choirs still performed in churches with a divided chancel, compositions that required antiphonal singing in anthems became less common. Solos were shorter and more accessible to amateur singers, and extremes of vocal range were avoided. The merging of cathedral and parish traditions was also a catalyst for a flourishing of pedagogical writings, usually published with the intention of educating choirmasters and singers in smaller parishes. Anglican chant continued to be performed in both large cathedrals and small parishes. Samuel Sebastian Wesley emerged as the greatest Anglican composer of the mid-nineteenth century.

The York Decision of 1820 (which will be discussed in chapter 5) established the legality of hymns in worship—a significant event in the history of Anglican church music. From this point forward, music-making would tend to be more congregational in nature, as the modern Anglican worship style began to take shape. In 1861, *Hymns Ancient and Modern* was published, and the practice of writing and singing treble descants for hymns grew. Organists began improvising in services as well. Several of the greatest English composers of the era devoted their energies to hymn writing, including Ralph Vaughan Williams, who is represented by more hymn tunes and arrangements in *The Hymnal 1982* than any other composer. Two other significant hymn collections soon followed: *The Yattendon Hymnal* of 1899 and *The English Hymnal* in 1906. In addition to Wesley, Stainer, Ouseley, and Vaughan Williams, many of the greatest masters of Anglican Church flourished or began their careers during the golden era from 1830 to 1922, including Edward Elgar, Herbert Howells, and Gerald Finzi. Although styles change and new music continues to be written, a glance through the index of *The Hymnal 1982* and standard anthem anthologies suggests the importance of this era to Episcopal church music.

Modern English Church Music: 1922–Present

The aftermath of World War I saw the rise of a more cynical and church-weary England, with church attendance shrinking rapidly. In 1922, a commission on church music published a report entitled *Music in Worship,* which stated that "the ideal in all parish churches is congregational singing." Hymn festivals began to flourish, and efforts were made to make liturgical "style" more family-friendly.

As the twentieth century progressed, some English composers began to experiment with musical styles as well. One landmark experiment was the "Twentieth Century Folk Mass" by Geoffrey Beaumont, which was premiered in 1956. In general, smaller parishes in England are less bound to tradition and more likely to experiment with alternate liturgies and absorb ecumenical styles that fall outside the Anglican tradition. The unified golden era has perhaps once again given way to the two distinct traditions of the cathedral and small parish.

Episcopal (American) Musical Traditions

The Episcopal Church in North America can trace its roots to 1607 with the founding of the Jamestown colony in Virginia. Robert Hunt celebrated the first known Eucharist in the New World. In 1624, Virginia became a royal colony and was required to conform to the Church of England, including weekly prayers for the King. In 1701, Thomas Bray founded the Society for the Propagation of the Gospel in Maryland, sparking the growth and spread of the Church of England throughout the colonies. Following the Declaration of Independence in 1776, many Anglican priests fled to England or Canada. The Revolutionary War officially ended in 1783 with the signing of the Treaty of Paris, and Samuel Seabury was consecrated by bishops of the Scottish Episcopal Church as the first American bishop in 1784. The Protestant Episcopal Church was founded in 1789, and the first American Book of Common Prayer (a revision of the 1662 prayer book) was published in the same year.

Throughout most of its history, the music of the Episcopal Church has been remarkably similar to the music of the Church of England. American choirmasters and organists largely performed the same repertoire by the same composers. However, from the Episcopal Church's earliest days, hymnody was emphasized to a greater extent, due to an American prioritization of congregational singing. The English collection *Hymns Ancient and Modern,* first published in 1861, had considerable influence on the music of the Episcopal Church, as did two other British publications: *The Yattendon Hymnal* (1899) and *The English Hymnal* (1906).

The first four Episcopal hymnals in the United States—authorized in 1789, 1826, 1871, and 1892, respectively—consisted only of authorized words. In 1913, the Joint Commission on the Revision of the Hymnal produced the first Episcopal hymnal consisting of both words and music. Simply entitled *The Hymnal,* this work is now retroactively known as *The Hymnal 1916.* In 1919, the Joint Commission on Church Music was formed, the deliberations of which resulted in the eventual publication of *The Hymnal 1940.* This hymnal was conceived to be used in tandem with the 1928 revision of the Book of Common Prayer. After the publication of the 1979 Book of Common Prayer, the hymnal was revised once again, resulting in the publication of *The Hymnal 1982.* This hymnal, perhaps more than any of its predecessors, emphasizes the importance of congregational singing.

QUESTIONS FOR REFLECTION AND DISCUSSION

1. Episcopal church music is historically indebted to the Church of England. Does the parish you attend draw from that Anglican tradition? Which period(s) in particular? Are there any non-Anglican traditions your church explores?

2. Contemporary Episcopal liturgy usually includes both choral offerings and congregational singing. What kind of "balance" do you think should exist within a single service? Are you the type of person who prefers to participate actively as a singer, or do you enjoy listening to the choir sing an anthem or psalm setting? (Or both?)

The Musical Structure of Worship in the Episcopal Church

The Church's one foundation
    is Jesus Christ her Lord;
she is his new creation
    by water and the word:
from heaven he came and sought her
    to be his holy bride;
with his own blood he bought her,
    and for her life he died.

Hymn 525, Stanza 1 (AURELIA)

The structure of the liturgy in the Episcopal Church is prescribed by the Book of Common Prayer. Since common prayer is a distinguishing feature of the Episcopal Church—and the entire Anglican Communion for that matter—a large church in New York City and a small country parish in northern Minnesota will follow the liturgical forms in ways that are strikingly similar to one another, even though the musical forces employed by the two are likely to be very different.

It is perhaps not surprising that a denomination bound by common prayer appreciates the commonalities of its musical heritage as well. While stylistic diversity within the music of the Episcopal Church can be found, a surprising number of churches still maintain a strong allegiance to Anglican musical traditions. This chapter will outline the structure of the Eucharist in preparation for our overview of *The Hymnal 1982,* a companion volume to the 1979 Book of Common Prayer and the official hymnal of the Episcopal Church.

How Much Music Should There Be? (High versus Low Church)

On the surface, this may seem like a silly question, but it is actually an important one. While the Book of Common Prayer is very specific in its assignment of specific texts to be used throughout the liturgy, it says surprisingly little about music. In fact, no music is necessary at all in the celebration of the Eucharist. However, while it is permissible and valid to celebrate the Eucharist or pray a daily office that contains no music, this is not the norm. Most Episcopal liturgies contain *a lot* of music, a quality that is the result of both tradition and an underlying principle in our prayer book: "Where rubrics indicate that a part of a service is to be 'said,' it must be understood to include 'or sung,' and *vice versa*" (BCP 14).

Sometimes clergy actively involve themselves in the music-making, singing the various responses and collects as outlined in the Book of Common Prayer. This kind of liturgy is generally referred to as "high church." To church musicians, a high church style broadly (and colloquially) translates to "a lot of music." In high church liturgies, virtually everything is sung, with the exception of the readings and the sermon. The congregation may even sing the Nicene Creed and the Lord's Prayer. The opposite extreme is "low church." These liturgies are either entirely spoken or contain very little music, perhaps only a hymn or two. There is, of course, the entire spectrum of parishes between these two extremes and all approaches are equally valid. Most churches find a middle ground, and this chapter assumes that middle ground. The following pages will outline the music that one might hear in a Sunday Eucharist at an average-sized Episcopal Church, with about a hundred thirty people in the pews on a given Sunday.

WHO CHOOSES THE MUSIC?

While the priest is responsible for all aspects of a parish's worship life, including the selection of music in the liturgy, many parishes designate a principal musician who participates in this responsibility for planning and oversight. The principal musician coordinates the selection of hymns, anthems, and service music along with the priest and, depending on the size of the parish, also supervises the musical staff, including professional singers, guest soloists, and instrumentalists, and manages special musical events, such as Lessons and Carols. Thus, in addition to having the requisite musical training, he or she must also have excellent leadership qualities and keen organizational and logistical skills.

> It shall be the duty of every Minister to see that music is used as an offering for the glory of God and as a help to the people in their worship in accordance with The Book of Common Prayer and as authorized by the rubrics or by the General Convention of this Church. To this end the Minister shall have final authority in the administration of matters pertaining to music. In fulfilling this responsibility the Minister shall seek assistance from persons skilled in music. Together they shall see that music is appropriate to the context in which it is used.[2]

Most priests recognize that their principal musician is an expert in his or her field, and will give that person considerable breadth and authority when choosing music. In turn, good music ministers respect their priests and will strive to work with him or her to create a liturgy appropriate to the day, season, and parish. Good teamwork and collegiality between the clergy and the music staff is essential to a vibrant and functional music program.

THE MUSICAL STRUCTURE OF THE EUCHARIST

Although the Book of Common Prayer designates that any part of the liturgy may be sung, most parishes maintain a balance of spoken versus sung portions of the liturgy.

The Prelude (or Preludes)

A prelude serves as an introduction. In music, preludes occur before any another piece of music, the latter of which serves as the main event. Johann Sebastian Bach, for instance, wrote many "preludes and fugues" that were intended to be performed as pairs. In worship, an instrumentalist may play one or more preludes before the liturgy begins, usually during the ten minutes prior. These selections serve as a prelude to the entire liturgy in general, and to the processional hymn in particular. Preludes before worship provide an opportunity for prayer and reflection as the community gathers.

The Processional Hymn

With the exception of certain penitential services (such as during Lent or Good Friday), the liturgy will often begin with a robust processional hymn. The term "processional hymn" is descriptive, as the choir—along with the crucifer, verger, acolytes, and clergy—will usually process down the center aisle as the congregation joins in singing. On major feast days, such as Easter or Pentecost, the choir may execute a more elaborate processional pattern, perhaps encircling the nave more than once before proceeding to the chancel area or choir loft. By the end of the processional hymn, the choir will have made its way to the chancel area or choir loft (depending on the architecture of the building).

The Gloria (or Trisagion or Kyrie)

The next musical moment of the Eucharist varies from season to season, and sometimes even from Sunday to Sunday. During Ordinary Time, Christmas, Epiphany, and Easter, a *Gloria* (Canticle 20, *Gloria in excelsis*) is usually sung before the first lesson is read. During Advent and Lent, however, the *Gloria* is replaced by either the less festive *Trisagion* or the penitential *Kyrie eleison* (usually during Lent only). The *Kyrie* is particularly suitable to Lenten services that begin with the Decalogue, which may also be sung. Eucharistic services that incorporate special liturgies, such as the sacrament of Holy Baptism, may omit the *Gloria* altogether with no replacement text or music.

The Psalm

Perhaps no part of an Episcopal liturgy is as thoroughly Anglican as the praying of the psalm. While it is permissible to read the psalm—the Book of Common Prayer always permits the option of speaking—it is contrary to the very nature of the psalms, which were composed in their original Hebrew with the intention of being sung. In fact, the English word "psalm" comes from the Greek word *psalmoi,* which means "instrumental music" or "the words accompanying the music." Thus, psalms should be sung whenever possible. In the Anglican tradition, psalms may be sung in a distinct and idiomatic style known as Anglican chant. Complex psalm formulas are usually sung by the choir alone, while simpler formulas invite congregational participation. Anglican chant may be the most common method of psalm singing, but there are many other options as well. (Psalmody will be discussed in depth in chapter 7.)

The Sequence Hymn

This congregational hymn is sung immediately before the reading of the Gospel. As this hymn is being sung, the bishop, priest, or deacon assigned to read the Gospel lesson will usually process down the center aisle, accompanied by a small group of acolytes. The sequence hymn is often related to the Gospel and also provides accompaniment for the liturgical action. After the sequence hymn is completed, one of the acolytes generally holds the Gospel as the ordained person reads.

The Offertory Anthem

Immediately following the Gospel is the sermon, which is then followed by the Nicene Creed, the Prayers of the People, Confession of Sin, and the Peace. After the Peace, the ministers and people greet one another, after which the presider speaks an offertory sentence (or sentence from scripture) to mark the beginning of the Offertory.

While the Book of Common Prayer allows a psalm or hymn to be sung during the Offertory, this is the most common place to insert an anthem sung by the choir alone. The anthem is picked to amplify the Gospel or one of the other lessons. The text of the anthem may be printed in the service bulletin. This is particularly important if the choir is singing a complicated polyphonic setting which—while beautiful in its musical form—can obscure the clarity of the text.

The Presentation Hymn

The Offertory concludes with a congregational presentation hymn. Depending on the parish, an entire hymn may be sung, or just one stanza of a hymn may be offered. Ideally, the text of the presentation hymn should complement the act of gift-giving, highlighting the fact that the people are offering their oblations to God.

It is worth noting that, in many churches, a doxology (a song of praise, such as "Praise God from whom all blessings flow") is sung here. Liturgically speaking, a doxology is part of the Eucharistic Prayer, not a presentation hymn at all. So while the text is not inappropriate, it may not be the best liturgical choice for this moment in the service.

The Sanctus and Fraction Anthem

During the Eucharistic Prayer, in both high and low church celebrations and everything in between, two portions of the text are usually sung. The *Sanctus* ("Holy, holy, holy Lord, God of power and might") is sung at the beginning of the Great Thanksgiving, immediately after the *Sursum corda*

("The Lord be with you") and presider's preface. While the text of the *Sanctus* is always the same, it is common practice for the musical setting to rotate according to season.

The fraction anthem is a congregational text sung immediately after the breaking of the bread. The *Agnus Dei* ("Lamb of God, you take away the sins of the world") is commonly used as the fraction anthem, but other texts (such as "Christ our Passover is sacrificed for us") are appropriate as well. Like the *Sanctus,* fraction anthems may be rotated according to season.

Music during Communion

Musically, this is perhaps the most flexible part of the Eucharist. The music offered as the people receive communion can take a variety of forms. Several congregational hymns are typically programmed, but these are generally quieter and more contemplative in nature than hymns during other portions of the service. A second choral anthem is sometimes scheduled at this time, and instrumental selections are commonly heard as well.

The Recessional Hymn

The recessional hymn is almost identical in character to the processional hymn. During this final hymn, the choir—again, along with the crucifer, verger, acolytes, and clergy—will process from the chancel area (or choir loft) toward the back of the nave, singing along with the congregation. Often, the choir surrounds the perimeter of church where they remain in place for the final stanza of the recessional hymn. Sometimes recessional hymns are also labeled as "processional hymns" (just like the opening hymn). While this may confuse matters a bit, it is indicative of the nature of these two moments; they parallel one another as the congregation now "processes" out to "love and serve the Lord."

The Postlude

The postlude begins immediately after the recessional hymn and final (usually spoken) dismissal. While there may be multiple selections offered as part of the prelude, the postlude usually consists of one piece. Most parishioners file out of the church during the postlude, but some remain quietly seated until the music concludes, both as a moment of enjoyment in listening to the music and as a gesture of respect for the organist.

WE HAVE HEARD WITH OUR EARS: OTHER MUSIC YOU MAY EXPERIENCE

While the above list highlights the most basic musical ingredients of a eucharistic liturgy, there are other elements that you may hear as well, all of which either augment one of the principal elements or musically enhance the service in some other way.

Descants

A descant is an alternate musical line that is sung or played above the melody line. While descants may be sung at a variety of times during the service, they are most frequently heard during the final stanzas of the processional and recessional hymns. Many choirmasters write their own descants, and there are published anthologies of descants as well. While descants are almost always sung by the trebles (or sopranos) of the choir, some descants are included in *The Hymnal 1982,* inviting congregational participation as well. During particular feast days such as Easter, an instrumental descant (often a trumpet) may be added. Descants are generally omitted during Lent.

Alternate Harmonizations

Sometimes, during the last stanza of a processional or recessional hymn, congregational singers may be surprised by what they hear from the organ. An alto, tenor, or bass may find that her or his harmonic line no longer "works" with what the organist is playing. These "alternate harmonizations" are deliberate and standard practice in the Episcopal Church. They are intended to increase the power of a final stanza, and the singers in the congregation and choir are expected to abandon their four-part harmony and all join in unison on the melody.

During this stanza, a descant may be added and the tempo may become a bit slower and more articulated in character. Skilled organists may also add some transitional material followed by a modulation (usually a whole step upward) immediately before the final stanza of a hymn. While there are many published volumes of alternate harmonizations available, it is not uncommon for an organist to write or "work out" his or her own alternate harmonizations. Occasionally, alternate harmonizations are heard on interior stanzas as well.

Organ Improvisations

Often, the organist will play transitional music between other musical numbers or liturgical events. For instance, a sequence hymn is generally sung as the bishop, priest, or deacon walks down the aisle before the Gospel reading, but after the reading the preacher may walk toward the pulpit accompanied by some improvised organ music. Organists may also provide transitional material in between communion hymns or between the offertory anthem and presentation hymn. While this music can be preplanned to an extent, it is not music that is "written down" or performed the same way each time. There is a considerable amount of spontaneity to it. Most organists become proficient with improvisation to some degree, and musical ideas that comprise improvisations usually come directly from material just heard, such as a tune from a hymn or anthem. Particularly prodigious or experienced organists may have the skill to improvise an entire piece of music worthy of standing alongside a composed piece of organ literature.

Instrumentalists

Episcopal churches often invite instrumentalists to participate in services. This is particularly true on feast days, such as Christmas, Easter, Ascension, or All Saints' Day. On Easter Day, for instance, it is not uncommon for a full brass ensemble to participate in the service. Sometimes, talented instrumentalists are members of the parish and may offer their gifts for the parish's worship. Some choir anthem accompaniments require an instrument (or instruments) in addition to organ. On Sundays when these anthems are scheduled, the instrumentalists may offer the prelude, postlude, or communion music.

SEASONS OF CHANGE

In addition to the prescribed liturgies outlined in the Book of Common Prayer, subtle (and not-so-subtle) changes in the music occur at different times throughout the church year. In fact, a good understanding of church music necessitates a thorough understanding of the seasons of the church year.[3]

A skilled musician is particularly gifted in bringing out the nuances of seasons through the choice of musical selections that highlight the atmosphere of a particular season. Choirmasters generally develop a "rotation" of service music to be used at different times throughout the church year. For instance, although the *Sanctus* and fraction anthems are used year-round, you will likely experience different settings in different seasons. Three or four distinct *Gloria*s are also necessary for those seasons in which a *Gloria* is appropriate: Ordinary Time, Christmas, Epiphany, and Easter. Presentation hymns are often rotated seasonally as well.

Some priests may also prefer—particularly during Lent— to have a quieter, more reflective tone; in other words, they may ask the music minister to deliberately program less music. The organ is commonly "silenced" to some degree during Lent. For instance, services might begin and end in silence rather than with a prelude or postlude. While this practice is not altogether uncommon, it is also somewhat unnecessary.

It is worth pointing out that virtually all of the great organ composers composed settings specifically for Lent, so it is always possible to acknowledge the change of season without silencing the instrument altogether. One particularly effective tradition, however, is to silence the organ completely in between the end of the Maundy Thursday service and Easter Vigil, which begins in darkness and silence until the organ triumphantly returns with the first "Alleluia" of Easter.

The church year has influence over non-musical considerations as well. For instance, many choirs abandon their white surpluses during Lent or Holy Week, or wear the colors of the liturgical season throughout the church year.

DIFFERENCES BETWEEN SMALL AND LARGE PARISHES (AND CATHEDRALS)

Good liturgical music carefully considers the architectural space in which the service occurs. While the size of a space is not an indicator of the size or quality of an organ, the organist and choirmaster must also carefully select repertoire that shows off the instrument to best advantage. Likewise, *a cappella* (unaccompanied) choral selections might not work as well in spaces that are not particularly resonant. The length of time necessary to complete the liturgical action is also considered. Attendance, as well as the number of clergy and lay servers, influences the length of communion and the number of musical selections needed for that portion of the service.

QUESTIONS FOR REFLECTION AND DISCUSSION

1. This chapter describes a Sunday morning Eucharist at a typical Episcopal church. Think about the church you attend most regularly. Does it fall neatly into this pattern, or has your experience been something different?

2. The next time you travel, deliberately seek out an Episcopal church to which you have never been before. Armed with the information in this chapter, reflect upon what you hear. Would you describe this church as "high church" or "low church"? Does it adhere to the Anglican traditions outlined in this chapter, or were there sounds that surprised you?

3. If you are not a cradle Episcopalian, what drew you to the Episcopal Church? If it was the music (either entirely or in part), what in particular fascinated you? Are there any non-Anglican traditions that you miss?

The Hymnal 1982: Introduction and Overview

We the Lord's people, heart and voice uniting,
praise him who called us out of sin and darkness
into his own light, that he might anoint us
a royal priesthood.

Hymn 51, Stanza 1 (DECATUR PLACE)

If you visit any Episcopal Church in the United States, you will probably find at least two books in every pew. The first one is (of course) the Book of Common Prayer, which is the bedrock of the denomination. The second is *The Hymnal 1982*. While other books—the Bible and supplemental hymnals such as *Lift Every Voice and Sing II, Wonder, Love, and Praise,* and *El Himnario*—can be found occasionally, these two volumes are by far the most common. It is no coincidence that *The Hymnal 1982* was adopted so soon after the 1979 Book of Common Prayer. The two books are companion volumes that shape modern Episcopal worship, and are even published in a single volume.

The Hymnal 1982 is so essential to an understanding of Episcopal church music that three chapters of this book will be devoted to it. This chapter will give an introduction and overview to the hymnal, discussing the book in its historical context, addressing its content in general, and mentioning supplemental companions that have been published since its release. The second chapter will be devoted entirely to the 288 pieces of service music included in the standard pew edition of *The Hymnal 1982*, and the third will discuss the 720 hymns. It is probably best to read these three chapters of this book with a copy of *The Hymnal 1982* at hand or downloaded on a tablet or other electronic device, so that you can refer to the musical examples discussed here.

THE IMPORTANCE OF CONGREGATIONAL SINGING

Congregational singing became more of a priority for the Episcopal Church over the course of the twentieth century, and the desire for greater participation in congregational singing was one of the principal ambitions behind the publication of *The Hymnal 1982*. Raymond F. Glover, in his superb short essay, "What Is Congregational Song?", describes congregational song as "the declaration of a people who have had an encounter with the living God":

> Further, in its performance we are bound together with countless numbers of those with whom we share this faith experience. Among them are not only the visible body of people with whom we gather for corporate worship, but also that invisible body of people who share our faith, but live and worship in other places. And even larger than all of these is that body of the saints who are present with us and who continue to sing their endless songs of praise and prayer around the throne of the "Lord of hosts Most High."[4]

To represent these multitudes, the editors of *The Hymnal 1982* deliberately included music that represented as many different eras, styles, and cultures as possible. In addition to the great hymnody of the Anglican tradition, tenth-century plainsong stands alongside Lutheran chorales; French, Scot-

tish, and English psalter tunes are included among folk songs
and other diverse music styles. Glover continues:

> The cultural diversity of the composers and of the sources of
> those tunes whose creators remain unknown provides us with
> a great variety of ways in which to perform our congrega-
> tional song.... As people living and worshiping in these latter
> years of the twentieth century, our congregational song is not
> only an expression of our faith, but it is also an identification
> of the fact that we are a people coming from many cultures
> and backgrounds. It reflects the diversity of our educational
> experience, the wide span of our ages and the various ways
> in which we worship God.[5]

Perhaps most important—following in the tradition of the
1539 Great Bible and the original 1549 Book of Common
Prayer almost five hundred years ago—*The Hymnal 1982* is
the people's book, an invitation for *all* to worship, as it concludes in its preface: "*The Hymnal 1982* is truly a book of and
for the people, reflecting their involvement in its creation and
responding to their desire for new songs with which to praise
God. May God prosper this handiwork!"

THE HYMNAL 1940:
A PRECURSOR TO THE HYMNAL 1982

Over the course of its long history, the Episcopal Church has
sanctioned a series of hymnals for use in worship. These volumes—seven in total—were authorized in 1789, 1826, 1871,
1892, 1916, 1940, and 1982. The first four, however, only
consisted of authorized words. From 1916 onward, the hymnals were prepared with music that was compiled and edited
by the Joint Commission on Church Music (which was later
renamed the Standing Commission on Church Music in 1973
and then in 1997 merged with the liturgy commission to become the Standing Commission on Liturgy and Music we
have today).

Thus, *The Hymnal*—which was first published as *The New Hymnal* and which we now retroactively call *The Hymnal 1916*—was the first music edition sanctioned by the Episcopal Church. It drew heavily upon preexisting sources, especially the English collection *Hymns Ancient and Modern,* which had been first published in 1861, with many subsequent revisions. *The Hymnal 1916* included 561 hymns and thirty-one pieces of service music, many of them from its Church of England forerunner, *Hymns Ancient and Modern.* It was *The Hymnal 1916* that standardized many of the tunes that we now associate with specific hymn texts.

In 1928 the Book of Common Prayer was revised, and the Episcopal Church began thinking of updating the hymnal to conform to the new language. At the General Convention of 1937, the Joint Commission on Church Music was given the duty of preparing a new edition of the hymnal.

> The Commission began its work upon the principle "Prove all things; hold fast that which is good." Every hymn in the Hymnals of 1892 and of 1916 was read with care and criticized from the viewpoints of reality, religious feeling, literary worth, and usefulness, and those which met these tests were retained.[6]

The result was *The Hymnal 1940.* In their essay "The Publication of the Hymnal of the Episcopal Church," Leonard L. Ellinwood and Charles G. Manns detail the content of new hymnal—both the texts and the music—in comparison to its predecessor:

> While the majority of the texts finally accepted were hymns of American and British authors, there were eighty-one translations from Latin, twenty-five from Greek, forty-five from German, three each from Dutch and Italian, two each from French and Hebrew, and single ones from Danish, Irish, Swahili, Syriac, and Welsh.... In preparing the music edition, to fit the historical span of texts, tunes were drawn from the

entire history of music: from the sixth century down to selections from the nearly five thousand tunes that were sub-
mitted anonymously. More harmonizations of J. S. Bach as
well as more early American camp meeting and folk melodies
were included. There were 100 pages of service music, so that
the volume fully equipped any church for every essential need
of its musical worship.[7]

The Hymnal 1940 also emphasized congregational singing,
and introduced sacred folk tunes from the United States, England, Ireland, Scandinavia, the Netherlands, Germany, and
France, plus forty-eight new tunes by American and Canadian
composers. The hymnal was widely acclaimed by church musicians and quickly adopted in Episcopal churches throughout
the United States.

Over forty years would pass before the Episcopal Church
would issue its next hymnal. While there are substantial differences, the format of *The Hymnal 1940* significantly influenced the form and content of *The Hymnal 1982*.

THE CREATION OF *THE HYMNAL 1982*

The publication of the 1979 Book of Common Prayer was a
watershed moment in the history of the Episcopal Church. As
the work of prayer book revision was being done throughout
the 1970s, it was widely acknowledged that a hymnal revision
would soon follow out of necessity to conform to the new
liturgy. At the 1979 General Convention, Resolution A–69
directed the Standing Commission on Church Music "to present to the 1982 General Convention a collection of hymn
texts for an enriched and up-dated Hymnal."

Although *The Hymnal 1940* was intended for use with the
1928 Book of Common Prayer, even more synergy exists between *The Hymnal 1982* and the 1979 Book of Common
Prayer. A joint examination of their respective tables of contents reveals the parallel organization of the two books. The
Joint Commission on Church Music also acknowledged how

much the world had changed over the past several decades (particularly during the 1960s and 1970s), and many felt that the new sociological climate calling for greater ecumenism, social equality, and liturgical renewal required the contents of the hymnal to be reexamined.

When compiling *The Hymnal 1982,* the Standing Commission on Church Music developed the following objectives:

- to prepare a body of texts that presents the Christian faith with clarity and integrity;
- to restore music which has lost some of its melodic, rhythmic, or harmonic vitality through prior revision;
- to reflect the nature of today's Church by including the works of contemporary artists and works representing many cultures;
- to strengthen ecumenical relationships through the inclusion of texts and tunes used by other Christian traditions;
- to create a hymnal embodying both practicality and esthetic excellence.[8]

The result was a hymnal that strove to retain the best of the past while simultaneously modernizing the language and becoming more gender-neutral and culturally inclusive. New hymns and service music were also incorporated (some of them via special commissions), and multiculturalism became a much greater priority.

The long life of *The Hymnal 1940* resulted in the issue of many supplemental volumes that provided service music settings and other material not found in the original hymnal. One of the practical goals of *The Hymnal 1982* was to issue all of these resources at once through the service music appendix found in the full accompaniment edition of *The Hymnal 1982,* and it is unquestionably far more comprehensive in nature than any previous hymnal.

TYPES OF MUSIC FOUND IN *THE HYMNAL 1982*
The Hymnal 1982 contains a greater variety of music than any of its predecessors, from Gregorian chant to contemporary popular religious songs. These tunes and their harmonizations have their origins in a wide variety of sources, and include a number of different musical genres.

Homophonic Hymn Settings
These are the standard four-part settings that most readily come to mind when people hear the word "hymn." These standard hymn settings permeate *The Hymnal 1982*. "Homophonic" refers to the texture of the music—multiple parts simultaneously singing in the same rhythm. The earliest of these homophonic settings have their origin as Lutheran chorale tunes; the tune names of these hymns usually retain their German names. Most of the other four-part settings in *The Hymnal 1982* come from the later Protestant tradition, including many hymns from the Anglican and American tradition.

Metrical Settings of a Tune
This broad category refers to hymns consisting of a single melodic line that—unlike plainchant—are set to an exact meter or rhythm. The earliest of these settings in *The Hymnal 1982* come from the Lutheran tradition; see "O Sacred Head, Sore Wounded" (HERZLICH TUT MICH VERLANGEN, 169) and "A Mighty Fortress Is Our God" (EIN FESTE BURG, 687). "Come, Thou Fount of Every Blessing" (NETTLETON, 686) is a more modern example. Many pieces of service music in *The Hymnal 1982* also fall into this metrical category, such as the Rite II *Venite* found at S35.

Folk Songs
Every country has a rich tradition of folk songs. One of the innovations of *The Hymnal 1982* is its incorporation of folk song melodies from many different cultures, including those from world cultures beyond Europe and the United States.

This multicultural aspect of *The Hymnal 1982* will be discussed in greater detail below.

Rounds and Canons

Canons (or rounds, in the colloquial/folk sense) occur when the same melody is sung or played at two or more different (but fixed) time intervals, thus creating a more complex and imitative composition. "Row, Row, Row Your Boat" is a popular example of a round/canon. Tunes that work as canons can also be sung in unison. Some of the selections in *The Hymnal 1982* can be performed as rounds or canons, such as THE EIGHTH TUNE (25), WYNGATE CANON (254), and PURPOSE (534). A collection of six rounds and canons is also gathered at the end of the hymnal (Hymns 710–715).

Plainchant

Plainchant has its origins in the Gregorian chants used in the pre-Reformation church beginning in the ninth century. These chants are performed freely, following the natural rise and fall of the declamatory vocal line and without regard to a particular meter. Occasionally, vertical lines are inserted above selected notes to indicate stressed syllables (see, for example, CAELITUM JOSEPH, 283). Although these chants generally set English texts in *The Hymnal 1982*, most of these chant-based hymns retain the name of the original Latin chant in their hymn tune name. There are many examples of plainchant throughout *The Hymnal 1982*, particularly in the service music section of the hymnal.

Anglican Chant

Anglican chant is a unique tradition of using harmonized formulas for singing psalms and canticles. Anglican chant formulas usually consist of a series of homophonic chords that can be used interchangeably with various psalm texts. The psalms (or canticles) are then "pointed" (reconciled with the selected formula), often by the choirmaster or organist. The standard Anglican chant is a "double chant," which consists of two phrases of ten chords each; each phrase can be broken into two smaller subphrases (4 chords + 6 chords). Single chants (one phrase) are also utilized with some degree of regularity, and—on rare occasions—triple chants (three phrases) are used as well. Anglican chant is one of the Episcopal Church's proudest musical traditions, and examples can be found throughout the Morning Prayer and Canticles service music collections in *The Hymnal 1982*; *The Anglican Chant Psalter* also provides an additional 361 formulas.

MULTICULTURALISM IN *THE HYMNAL 1982*

While *The Hymnal 1940* was a landmark achievement, the creators of *The Hymnal 1982* made a conscious effort to be more culturally inclusive in their hymn selections. The final collection included eight songs from African-American culture (Hymns 99, 172, 325, 468, 529, 599, 648, and 676); four from the Judaic tradition (Hymns 393, 425, 536, and 714); two from Hispanic cultures (Hymns 113 and 277); two work songs from Africa (Hymns 602 and 611); two folk songs from China (Hymns 340 and 342); a Native American folk song (Hymn 385); a French folk tune (Hymn 114); and an Eastern Orthodox Slavonic chant (Hymn 355). Many of these hymns are now widely known in parishes throughout the Episcopal Church, such as "Let Us Break Bread Together on Our Knees" (Hymn 325) and "There Is a Balm in Gilead" (Hymn 676). They have also made Episcopalians more aware of the many diverse cultures that are part of the Anglican tradition, and stimulated a hunger for more hymns that bring those cultures into Episcopal worship.

SUPPLEMENTS TO *THE HYMNAL 1982*

While *The Hymnal 1982* largely had been well received, its one-volume size also came with certain limitations. In the decades following the publication of the hymnal, the Episcopal Church released five additional volumes that were meant to be official companions of and supplements to *The Hymnal 1982*. Each of these collections revolved around a particular theme and efforts to expand and modernize the liturgy, as well as to address needs not adequately covered by *The Hymnal 1982*.

These supplemental volumes include *Lift Every Voice and Sing II* (1993), *Wonder, Love, and Praise* (1997), *El Himnario* (2001), *Voices Found* (2003), and *My Heart Sings Out* (2004). All are still in print and recognized as official hymnals of the Episcopal Church. Like *The Hymnal 1982,* all of these books are intended for use in liturgical worship. Therefore, like the hymnal, the musical contents are categorized thematically and according to the church year so that hymns can be appropriately selected for use in worship.

Lift Every Voice and Sing II (1993)

This is a collection of 280 pieces from African American and Gospel traditions. The "II" in the title indicates that it is a sequel. It was preceded by a volume that was actually released before *The Hymnal 1982* entitled *Lift Every Voice and Sing: A Collection of Afro-American Spirituals and Other Songs* (1981). The original volume, although out of print, is commonly referred to as *Lift Every Voice and Sing I.*

Lift Every Voice and Sing II was compiled under the supervision of the Office of Black Ministries of the Episcopal Church. The creators were inspired by similar volumes in other denominations, most significantly the Methodist *Songs of Zion* (1981) and the Roman Catholic *Lead Me, Guide Me* (1987). It includes African-American spirituals, traditional and contemporary Gospel songs, adapted Protestant hymns, missionary and evangelistic hymns, and service music in alternative settings. With the exception of the title hymn ("Lift Every Voice and Sing"), *Lift Every Voice and Sing II* is an entirely new collection and avoids hymns that were already included in *The Hymnal 1982.*

Wonder, Love, and Praise (1997)
Beginning its numbering with Hymn 721, *Wonder, Love, and Praise* was conceived as an official addition to *The Hymnal 1982*. In fact, it is subtitled *A Supplement to The Hymnal 1982*. It was intended to provide "additional service music, inclusive language hymnody, additional texts in languages other than English, including texts printed in more than one language, additional hymnody related to the lectionary and rites of the Book of Common Prayer, and texts and tunes written since the compiling of the present Hymnal."[9]

Thus when compiling *Wonder, Love, and Praise,* the editorial committee followed three guiding principles: first, to prepare a resource that added to *The Hymnal 1982*; second, to strive for a musical simplicity that encourages immediate participation; and third, to offer a breadth of musical styles from many cultures. The result was an eclectic variety of 114 hymns and spiritual songs (Hymns 721–834) and 72 new pieces of service music (Hymns 835–906; the "S" designation before service music numbers is not used in this volume). The service music section is particularly interesting, containing 29 new canticle settings, including six settings of the *Gloria in excelsis* and two settings of *Te Deum laudamus*. In addition, there are 29 selections of devotional music, including table graces, rounds, acclamations, and selections from the Taizé community. The volume is permeated by a congregational philosophy of music-making:

> The church has entered a new frontier of inclusive hospitality, not only in welcoming all to the table, but also in providing rites, forms, and music which encourage the sharing of one's cultural story to foster the unity proclaimed in the gospel. This supplement honors that pilgrimage and affirms "the participation of all in the Body of Christ the Church, while recognizing our diverse natures as children of God."[10]

El Himnario (1998)

El Himnario is an ecumenical hymnal for Hispanic parishes. The Episcopal Church and several other mainline denominations sponsored this volume. In 2001, *El Himnario Selecciones* was released. This collection is an inexpensive, words-only edition of favorite hymns and songs from the original *El Himnario* alongside translations of other hymns familiar to Hispanic congregations.

Voices Found (2003)

Subtitled *Women in the Church's Song, Voices Found* is "a rich collection of hymns and spiritual songs by, for, and about women."[11] Most of the music is written in a congregational style and is intended for normal parish use. While some of the selections are written in traditional four-part harmony, many are in unison or two parts, making them especially appropriate to be sung entirely by women. According to the preface, *Voices Found* "is a unique compilation of contemporary and historical materials that crosses boundaries of geography, time, and culture as it represents the diversity of the gifts of women and seeks to affirm and expand the spirituality of all women and men as they find new voices in the church's song."

My Heart Sings Out (2004)

My Heart Sings Out is a hymnal designed for inclusive worship for people of all ages. Its specific goal is the full inclusion of younger children in weekly worship. It is organized into two main sections—the eucharistic liturgy and the church year—with additional thematic sections, including songs for baptism and confirmation, songs of thanks and praise, and songs of suffering, healing, and assurance. The melodies are age-appropriate and the selections offer opportunities for adults to sing their parts in harmony, joining alongside the children's voices.

WHEN WILL THE EPISCOPAL CHURCH ADOPT A NEW HYMNAL?

Eventually the Episcopal Church will no doubt sanction another revision of the hymnal, but it will probably not be happening soon. In recent years the church has considered the idea, and in 2011 an official survey by the Church Pension Group Office of Research was conducted entitled "The Hymnal Revision Feasibility Study." The survey considered questions of whether Episcopalians perceived a need for a new hymnal, the importance of music in the life and faith of the congregation, the ways in which music attracts new members to the church, and what formats are most effective for delivering the musical resources congregations need.

The results of the study were very informative and somewhat surprising. After analyzing the data, the committee reported that while clergy and music directors tended to favor hymnal revision, most church members were opposed. Some of the reasons were financial concerns related to the purchasing of new hymnals, but many respondents considered *The Hymnal 1982* to be a key aspect of the Episcopal Church's identity, defining what it means to be "grounded within the Anglican tradition." The committee concluded that because *The Hymnal 1982* has become so central to the life of the Episcopal Church, "a rush to revise the hymnal could seriously undermine and weaken the Church, alienating those who have remained with the Episcopal Church through difficult times."[12]

Forty-two years passed between the publication of *The Hymnal 1940* and *The Hymnal 1982*. Given the results of "The Hymnal Revision Feasibility Study," it seems unlikely that the Episcopal Church will commission a new official hymnal by 2024, when another forty-two years will have lapsed. But—if history tells us anything—it seems equally unlikely that *The Hymnal 1982* will *never* be revised. It is hard to imagine that a congregation in 2082 would be satisfied using a resource containing nothing from their century, the entire content of which was written before any of the congregants were even born. Surely a twenty-first-century hymnal, or some other musical resource, will be produced. The only questions are when and in what format.

Q QUESTIONS FOR REFLECTION
AND DISCUSSION

1. How important is congregational singing to you? Do you like to actively participate in the musical aspects of a worship service, or do you consider yourself to be more of a listener? How important is singing to your worship experience?

2. Have you ever used any of the five supplements to *The Hymnal 1982* in worship? If so, which one(s)? Did you enjoy your experience? How regularly does your church utilize these resources?

3. *The Hymnal 1982* is over thirty years old. Do you feel that it is still relevant? Why or why not? Are you in favor of a future hymnal revision? If so, when would you like to see it occur, and what would like it to include?

The Hymnal 1982:
Service Music

Come, let us sing to the Lord;
    let us shout with joy to the Rock of our salvation.
Let us come before his presence with thanksgiving,
    and raise a loud shout to him with psalms.
For the Lord is a great God,
    and a great King above all gods.
In his hand are the caverns of the earth,
    and the heights of the hills are his also.
The sea is his, for he made it,
    and his hands have molded the dry land.
Come, let us bow down and bend the knee,
    and kneel before the Lord our Maker.

The Invitatory: Venite,
Morning Prayer Rite II, S34–S40

Service music comprises the first part of *The Hymnal 1982*. The term "service music" refers to musical settings of texts from the liturgies in the Book of Common Prayer, in contrast with hymns, which are religious texts not found in the prayer book. In virtually all cases, the texts of service music are specifically prescribed by the liturgy, whereas hymns and their texts are chosen to augment the liturgy.[13] The pew edition of *The*

Hymnal 1982 contains 288 pieces of service music that are numbered sequentially. To avoid confusion with hymns, an "S" precedes each service music number (S110, S277, and so on).

SINGING THE BOOK OF COMMON PRAYER

Singing is not required in Episcopal worship. However, while any text from the Book of Common Prayer can be spoken, all-spoken services are generally not the primary liturgy in most parishes. The service music section of *The Hymnal 1982* invites the congregation to participate in sung settings of the liturgy. While the Book of Common Prayer only includes one version of any given text, *The Hymnal 1982* usually provides multiple musical settings for that text. It is the job of the rector, in consultation with the music minister, to select appropriate settings for congregational use in his or her parish. There are of course many other settings of these texts in addition to those published in *The Hymnal 1982,* but this chapter will focus only on the settings published in that volume.

The service music in *The Hymnal 1982* is arranged in six large sections:

- ◆ The Daily Office (S1–S66)
- ◆ The Great Litany (S67)
- ◆ Proper Liturgies for Special Days (S68–S70)
- ◆ Holy Baptism (S71–S75)
- ◆ The Holy Eucharist (S76–S176)
- ◆ Canticles (S177–S288).

As a comparison of this list with the table of contents to the Book of Common Prayer will show, the organization of the service music section of the hymnal is intimately related to and in fact almost mirrors the organization of the Book of Common Prayer. The minor differences are easily explained. *The Hymnal 1982* does not have a section devoted to collects, as these passages are not congregational and always spoken (or sometimes intoned) by the priest. Conversely, the canticles are almost always sung portions of the service—either by the choir or congregation—and are thus gathered into one section of the hymnal for organizational convenience.

Out of the remaining sections of the Book of Common Prayer, only the Psalter (or Psalms) is traditionally sung in Anglican worship. Psalm tones—the various chants used to sing the psalms—appear in the accompanist's edition of the hymnal but not in the pew edition. The various tones may be used with any of the psalms. Some parishes use a single psalm tone exclusively over the years; others may use different tones in different liturgical seasons. Other metrical settings of the psalms, including Psalm 95 and Psalm 100, which are regularly included in Morning Prayer and will be discussed below, appear throughout the hymnal. It would be quite impossible to include all 150 psalms in the hymnal, and unnecessary since they appear in the Book of Common Prayer. *The Anglican Chant Psalter* (1987) and many other psalm collections fill in those gaps. (Psalm singing will be covered in greater depth in chapter 7.)

THE DAILY OFFICE (S1–S66)

The first part of the service music section of *The Hymnal 1982* is devoted to the daily office. As discussed in chapter 1, one of the principal reforms of the early Anglican Church was the development of two daily prayer offices from the eight offices of the monastic tradition. The 1979 Book of Common Prayer retains this recognition of two principal offices—Morning Prayer and Evening Prayer—with additional rites for Noonday (BCP 103) and Compline (BCP 127). *The Hymnal 1982* offers musical settings for the sung portions of Morning Prayer and Evening Prayer, both Rite I ("traditional" language) and Rite II ("contemporary" language) options provided, as well as hymns for Noonday and Compline. Thus, the Daily Office section of service music is divided into five parts:

◆ Daily Morning Prayer: Rite I (S1–S25)
◆ Daily Evening Prayer: Rite I (S26–S32)
◆ Daily Morning Prayer: Rite II (S33–S55)
◆ An Order of Worship for the Evening (S56–S57)
◆ Daily Evening Prayer: Rite II (S58–S66).

Daily Morning Prayer: Rite I (S1–S25)
This section offers musical settings of the following portions
of the Rite I version of Morning Prayer: the *Preces, Venite,*
Psalm 95, *Jubilate, Pascha nostrum,* Salutation and The Lord's
Prayer, Suffrages A and B, and the Concluding Versicle and
Response. Only two musical genres are represented in this
opening portion: plainchant and Anglican chant. While it is
possible to sing all of the selections in plainchant, Anglican
chant settings are provided for the *Venite* (S4–S7), Psalm 95
(S9–10), the *Jubilate* (S12–S13), and the *Pascha nostrum*
(S17–S20). The *Venite* is a modified version of Psalm 95; it
incorporates verses 1–7 of Psalm 95 followed by verses 9 and
13 of Psalm 96. The *Jubilate,* on the other hand, is simply another name for Psalm 100; the two are identical titles for the
same four verses.

The *Venite*—one of the two principal canticles of Morning
Prayer—is of particular interest in *The Hymnal 1982,* as two
distinct Anglican chant formulas are presented as options: two
single chants (S4–S5) and two double chants (S6–S7). Thus,
congregations have three options for singing the *Venite,* as
there is also a version in plainchant (S2–S3). Six settings in
three varieties (of varying levels of complexity) highlight the
importance of this canticle, which should always be sung if
possible.

One may reasonably question why two psalm settings—
Psalm 95 and the *Jubilate* (Psalm 100)—are included in the
Morning Prayer portion of the hymnal. These, in fact, are *The
Hymnal 1982's* only chant psalm settings. Although the cho-
rister or parishioner could simply refer to *The Anglican Chant
Psalter* during Morning Prayer when singing these two psalms,

they are included in *The Hymnal 1982* for practical reasons. While the lectionary prescribes rotating psalms for the Eucharist and Evening Prayer, Morning Prayer always includes these two psalms. Psalms may also be included as part of the readings assigned at Morning Prayer. Thus, they are included in the hymnal for convenience due to their frequent (daily) use during Morning Prayer.

The *Preces* ("O Lord, open thou our lips"), Salutation ("The Lord be with you / And with thy spirit"), Suffrages A ("O Lord, show thy mercy upon us"), and Suffrages B ("O Lord, save thy people, and bless thine heritage") are sung responsively in plainchant between the officiant and the people. The *Pascha nostrum* ("Christ our Passover is sacrificed for us") is sung by the congregation; in all seasons except Advent or Lent, an Alleluia antiphon is included. The Salutation and Lord's Prayer (if sung) are sung by everyone present on a monotone pitch. The concluding Versicle and Response ("Let us bless the Lord / Thanks be to God") is sung responsively in plainchant; alleluias are included during Eastertide (S25).

Settings of the *Te Deum laudamus* ("We Praise Thee")—the second principal canticle of Morning Prayer, along with the *Venite*—are located in the canticles section of *The Hymnal 1982*. The Rite I version appears in three settings (S205–S207).

Daily Evening Prayer: Rite I (S26–S32)

The section of service music for the daily office continues with musical settings of the following portions of the Rite I version of Evening Prayer, all of which are set to plainchant in *The Hymnal 1982*: the *Preces* (S26), *Phos hilaron* (S27), Salutation and The Lord's Prayer (S28), Suffrages B (S29–S30), and the Concluding Versicle and Response (S31–S32).

The *Phos hilaron* ("O Gracious Light") is an especially interesting text for musicians, as it is the earliest non-biblical Christian hymn still in use today. (Two other early Christian hymns—*Gloria in excelsis* and *Te Deum laudamus*—are also used regularly as canticles.) Originally written in New Testament (or *Koine*) Greek and frequently translated as "Hail Gladdening Light," the *Phos hilaron* has countless settings by both major and minor composers. Although a plainchant version appears in *The Hymnal 1982*, these manifold alternate settings of the *Phos hilaron* are frequently sung by the choir alone.

The Suffrages A are not included in the Evening Prayer service music section of *The Hymnal 1982* because they are identical to the Suffrages A of Morning Prayer (S22). Suffrages B, however, are different and included with the option of singing them on two different tones (S29 or S30). The *Preces* (S26) is set in plainchant, while the Salutation and Lord's Prayer (S28) and concluding Versicle and Response (S31–S32) are identical to those in the Morning Prayer settings (S21 and S24–S25).

The two principal canticles of Evening Prayer are the Song of Mary (*Magnificat*) and the Song of Simeon (*Nunc dimittis*). While there are congregational settings of these two texts in the canticles section of *The Hymnal 1982* (S185–S189 and S196–S200, respectively), there are also a multitude of magnificent choral settings by virtually every major Anglican composer from the Renaissance to the present day. As a result, these two canticles are almost always sung by the choir, who sing a paired "service"—*Magnificat* and *Nunc dimittis*—by a single composer. (These two canticles will be discussed in greater detail below, as well as in chapter 8.)

Daily Morning Prayer: Rite II (S33–S55)
This section of service music directly parallels S1–S25, offering Rite II versions of the same portions of Morning Prayer. While only two musical genres—plainchant and Anglican chant—were represented in the Rite I settings of Morning Prayer, this portion of the hymnal's service music offers a metrical setting of the *Venite* (S35). This version is an accessible

and appealing alternative for smaller parishes that are less accustomed to plainchant or Anglican chant.

An Order of Worship for the Evening (S56–S57)

This tiny section of service music—only two pieces—is the result of the 1979 prayer book revision, which includes an alternative order of worship that can be used in the evening. Both are distinct plainchant settings of the same greeting text. During Lent and Easter, they are replaced by the opening acclamation settings found in S78–S83.

Daily Evening Prayer: Rite II (S58–S66)

This section of service music directly parallels S26–S32, offering Rite II versions of the same portions of Evening Prayer. While only two musical genres—plainchant and Anglican chant—were represented in the Rite I settings of Evening Prayer, this portion of the hymnal offers two metrical settings of the *Phos hilaron* (S60–S61). Like the *Venite* of Morning Prayer, these metrical versions often work well to encourage congregational singing.

THE GREAT LITANY (S67)

According to the rubrics in the Book of Common Prayer, the Great Litany is "to be said or sung, kneeling, standing, or in procession; before the Eucharist or after the Collects of Morning or Evening Prayer; or separately; especially in Lent and on Rogation days" (BCP 148). Many parishes sing the Great Litany on the first Sunday of Lent to begin the penitential season. The Great Litany was composed in English by Archbishop Thomas Cranmer at the request of King Henry VIII, and predates the original Book of Common Prayer by five years (1544). It has been the tradition since the earliest days to sing the Great Litany in procession.

In *The Hymnal 1982*, the Great Litany appears in plainchant with no organ accompaniment. It is constructed in four sections: the invocation of the Trinity, the petitions (or deprecations), the supplications (or obsecrations), and the inter-cessions. After the Great Litany, the Book of Common Prayer also includes The Supplication, which is included in the sup-plemental section of service music in *The Hymnal 1982.*

PROPER LITURGIES FOR SPECIAL DAYS (S68–S70)
The service music pieces included in this brief section are all plainchant settings intended for use at the Great Vigil of Easter. The settings for the Palm Sunday liturgy texts are ac-tually located in the "Hymns" of *The Hymnal 1982,* numbers 153–157. (They will be discussed in chapter 5.)

HOLY BAPTISM (S71–S75)
All of these plainchant settings pertain to different aspects of the baptism service: the Opening Acclamation, Versicles, and the Litany and Thanksgiving over the Water. Three different acclamations are provided for use during Easter, Lent, and the rest of the church year.

THE HOLY EUCHARIST (S76–S176)
With the exception of the canticles, the section of service music devoted to the Holy Eucharist is the most extensive sin-gle section of *The Hymnal 1982.* This is understandable, as the Eucharist is the most frequently celebrated service in the Episcopal Church. For the sake of clarity, this large section of service music will be discussed here in smaller sections organ-ized by musical settings of the respective texts.

Opening Acclamation (S76–S83)
These eight selections are all settings of the opening acclama-tions found on pages 319 and 351 of the Book of Common Prayer. With the exception of S80 (which is a Rite I setting), all of these settings can be used for either Rite I or Rite II serv-ices. S78 and S79 are acclamations for Easter Day through the Day of Pentecost, whereas S81–S83 are acclamations for Lent.

Kyrie (S84–S98)

Kyrie eleison is a Greek text that translates "Lord, have mercy." It is appropriate for insertion at the conclusion of the Great Litany and Decalogue, and is often used as a substitution for the *Gloria* during Lent. Three options for the *Kyrie* are provided in the hymnal: S84–S89 set the Greek version, S90–S93 use the Rite I translation, and S94–S98 is the Rite II version. Settings range from plainsong to responsorial settings, and four-part and accompanied metric settings.

Trisagion (S99–S102)

Trisagion is a Greek word meaning "thrice holy." It is generally used in a similar fashion as the *Kyrie eleison* (as an alternative to the *Gloria* during Advent or Lent). It is also occasionally used during burial services.

The Nicene Creed (S103–S105)

Although usually spoken, *The Hymnal 1982* allows for the option of singing the Nicene Creed in plainchant (in both Rite I and Rite II). A metrical Rite II setting is also included (S105).

The Prayers of the People (S106–S109)

While the Prayers of the People are generally spoken, *The Hymnal 1982* includes sung options for Forms I, III, IV, and V, all in plainchant. Forms II and VI are included in the supplemental section of service music, but not in the standard pew edition.

The Peace (S110–S111) and Sursum corda (S112, S120)

The Hymnal 1982 makes these texts available in plainchant settings in Rite I and Rite II versions. The *Sursum corda* ("Lift up your hearts") is responsorial in nature.

Sanctus (S113–S117, S121–S131)

The *Sanctus* is perhaps the most frequently sung portion of the Eucharist. S113–S117 are the Rite I settings, and S121–

S131 are the Rite II versions. The Rite II settings by William Mathias (S128) and Robert Powell (S129) can be paired with their respective *Gloria in excelsis* settings found in the canticles section of the hymnal (S278 and S280). This is particularly effective during Christmas and Eastertide. Likewise the Franz Schubert setting of the *Sanctus* (S130, from his *Deutsche Messe*) may be paired with his *Kyrie* (S96) or *Agnus Dei* (S164) from the same work. Ultimately, however, complementary service music settings should selected and matched according to style and season, regardless of who composed them.

Conclusion of Eucharistic Prayer and Amen (S118, S142)
These are Rite I and Rite II settings in plainchant.

The Lord's Prayer (S119, S148–S150)
Although usually spoken, *The Hymnal 1982* allows for the option of singing the Lord's Prayer in plainchant (in both Rite I and Rite II). A four-part homophonic setting is also included (S150).

Memorial Acclamation (S132–S141)
Memorial acclamations, mostly set in plainchant with the exception of S135, are provided here for Eucharistic Prayers A, B, and D. The memorial acclamation for Prayer C is provided in the supplemental section of service music.

Amen (S143–147)
Five sung Amen settings are available in *The Hymnal 1982*. The first three (S143–S145) are plainsong settings and the last two are metrical (S146–S147). S144 and S145 are twofold settings as opposed to the more standard threefold versions (S143, S146–S47).

Fraction Anthems (S151–S172)
The fraction anthem is sung in response to the breaking of the bread during the Eucharist. Fraction anthems in *The Hym-*

nal 1982 are plentiful, with twenty-two distinct settings of a variety of texts, including the traditional *Agnus Dei*. They are grouped accordingly:

* Christ our Passover (S151–S156)
* *Agnus Dei*—Rite I (S157–S159)
* *Agnus Dei*—Rite II (S160–S163)
* Jesus, Lamb of God (S164–S166)
* The Disciples Knew the Lord Jesus (S167)
* My Flesh Is Food Indeed (S168–S169)
* Whoever Eats This Bread (S170)
* Be Known to Us (S171)
* Blessed Are Those Who Are Called (S172).

Responses (S173) and Dismissals (S174–S176)
These straightforward plainchant settings conclude the Eucharist. Alleluias are provided for dismissals during the Easter season.

CANTICLES (S177–S288)
Canticles are texts that function like psalms, but are not included among the 150 biblical psalms. Rather, they come from other sources, both biblical and non-biblical. Canticles have been a part of worship since the earliest days of Christianity, and are still often referred to by their Latin and Greek titles (even though they are sung in English in the contemporary Episcopal Church).

Canticles and their appearance in the Book of Common Prayer and hymnal can be confusing. Although there are twenty-one listed in the Book of Common Prayer, there are technically only fourteen, as seven are printed twice (in different translations). Appearing in both Rite I and Rite II versions, these same canticles are also assigned different numbers, which further complicates matters. The canticles are split between two different sections of the Book of Common Prayer: the Rite I versions appear on pages 47–53 and the Rite II versions on pages 85–96. Finally, for those congregations who do not offer sung Morning Prayer services regularly, the canticles can be somewhat unfamiliar; only one—the *Gloria in excelsis*—is sung with any frequency or regularity at a Sunday Eucharist. For this reason, some discussion of what the canticles are and how they function liturgically is necessary before discussing the musical contents of this extended section of service music.

The seven canticles that appear twice—in their Rite I and Rite II forms—include A Song of Creation (*Benedicite, omnia opera Domini*), A Song of Praise (*Benedictus es, Domine*), The Song of Mary (*Magnificat*), The Song of Zechariah (*Benedictus Dominus Deus*), The Song of Simeon (*Nunc dimittis*), Glory to God (*Gloria in excelsis*), and You are God (*Te Deum laudamus*). The fourteen distinct canticles can be discerned by recognizing that the first seven (BCP 47–53) are simply Rite I versions of later canticles; therefore, all of the distinct (Rite II) canticles are grouped in one place (BCP 85–96). Of these fourteen, nine are biblical: four from the Old Testament, three from the Gospel of Luke, and two from Revelation. The other five include three apocryphal passages and two ancient Christian hymns. The fourteen canticles will be briefly discussed below according to these literary groupings.

Old Testament Canticles (S208–S227)

These four canticles are taken from the books of Exodus and Isaiah. The Book of Common Prayer designates Canticle 8, The Song of Moses (*Cantemus Domino*), as being "especially suitable for use in Easter Season" (BCP 85). Taken from the fifteenth chapter of the book of Exodus, this canticle is the song that Moses and the Israelites sang after the Egyptians who were pursuing them drowned in the Red Sea. The other three Old Testament canticles are all from the book of Isaiah, and are designated as the First, Second, and Third Songs of Isaiah: *Ecce, Deus* (Canticle 9; BCP 86), *Quaerite Dominum* (Canticle 10; BCP 86), and *Surge, illuminare* (Canticle 11; BCP 87–88). All four of these canticles can be used on occasion after the Old Testament lesson during either Morning or Evening Prayer. *Surge, illuminare* is particularly appropriate for use during Advent.

Gospel Canticles (S185–S200; S242–S260)
Although usually referred to as "the Gospel canticles," they could just as accurately be called the "Canticles from Luke." The Song of Mary (*Magnificat*, Canticles 3 and 15; BCP 50 and 91–92) appears in the first chapter of Luke. Mary speaks these words to her cousin Elizabeth, who is pregnant with John the Baptist. Elizabeth praises Mary for her faith, and Mary responds with the *Magnificat*. Shortly thereafter, Zechariah (Elizabeth's husband) utters the *Benedictus Dominus Deus* (Canticles 4 and 16; BCP 50–51 and 92–93) upon the birth of his son; hence, this canticle is referred to as the Song of Zechariah. The final canticle—the Song of Simeon—is spoken by a devout Jew who had been promised that he would not die until he had seen the Savior. When Mary and Joseph visit the temple for the consecration of Jesus, Simeon holds the baby in his arms and speaks the *Nunc dimittis* (Canticles 5 and 17; BCP 51–52 and 93).

The three canticles are among the most important to liturgical worship. The *Magnificat* and the *Nunc dimittis* are the standard two canticles of Evening Prayer. Commonly joined together as the "short service," these two canticles are sung far more often than any others, with settings by virtually all of the major and minor Anglican composers. The *Benedictus Dominus Deus* is also one of the standard canticles of Morning Prayer, although it is often replaced by the *Jubilate* (Psalm 100).

Revelation Canticles (S261–S271)
These two canticles, both from the apocalyptic book of Revelation, can be used on certain non-feast offices of daily Morning Prayer. When used, they generally appear after the New Testament reading. The Song of the Redeemed (*Dignus es,*

Canticle 18; BCP 93–94) is sung by the twenty-four worship-ping elders before the throne of God. The Song of the Lamb (*Magna et mirabilia,* Canticle 19; BCP 94) is sung by the un-named warriors of chapter 15 who had conquered the beast.

Apocryphal Canticles (S177–S184; S228–S241)
Both A Song of Creation (*Benedicite, omnia opera Domini,* Canticles 1 and 12; BCP 47–49 and 88–90) and A Song of Praise (*Benedictus es, Domine,* Canticles 2 and 13; BCP 49 and 90) are from the Song of the Three Young Men. They are pas-sages in the Prayer of Azariah and the Song of the Three Jews, an addition to the book of Daniel included in the Apocrypha. The long poem from which these two excerpts are taken is a song of praise to God from the perspective of three children of God who have been condemned to burn in a fiery furnace. The *Kyrie Pantokrator*—the only canticle with a Greek title—also appears in an apocryphal book, the Prayer of Manasseh, which is included in an appendix to the Vulgate, a late fourth-century Latin edition of the Bible. Manasseh was King of Judah from 687–643 BCE. Like the four Old Testament can-ticles, all three of these apocryphal canticles can be can be used on occasion after the Old Testament lesson during either Morning or Evening Prayer.

Non-Biblical Canticles (S272–S288)
Like the *Phos hilaron* mentioned above, these final two canti-cles are early Christian hymns. Both are hymns of praise. The *Gloria in excelsis* (Canticles 6 and 20; BCP 52 and 94–95) is known as the Greater Doxology (as opposed to the *Gloria patri,* which is the Lesser Doxology) and is used in Morning Prayer as well as the Eucharist (except during Advent and Lent). The *Te Deum laudamus* (Canticles 7 and 21; BCP 52–53 and 95–96), originally ascribed to St. Ambrose and St. Au-gustine of Hippo, is one of the most important canticles of Morning Prayer, sung daily except during Lent.

Canticle Settings in *The Hymnal 1982*

In the service music section of *The Hymnal 1982*, the twenty-one canticles are presented in order as listed in the Book of Common Prayer. Thus, the Rite I canticles are grouped together (S177–S207), with the Rite II canticles immediately following them (S208–S288).

Although the canticles are commonly known by their Latin titles, all of the settings in *The Hymnal 1982* appear in English according to the translation found in the 1979 Book of Common Prayer. Although there have been subtle (and not-so-subtle) differences in their translations, the canticles have been sung almost exclusively in English since the 1549 prayer book and the very beginnings of the Anglican Church.

Most of the canticles in *The Hymnal 1982* are represented by a small number of settings. It is perhaps appropriate, however, that there are more settings of the *Gloria in excelsis* (fourteen total) than any other canticle, as this text is usually sung with more frequency than any other, particularly in smaller parishes that do not regularly offer Morning or Evening Prayer.

Supplemental Service Music (S289–S449)

Choirmasters and organists have access to an expanded version of *The Hymnal 1982*. This version is called the "accompaniment edition" to distinguish it from the standard pew edition. In addition to having full organ accompaniments to all service music and hymns (sometimes full accompaniments are not printed in the standard version), this version also includes 161 additional pieces of service music, many of which augment and complement the service music that appears as S1 through S289. These numbers include antiphons, alternate settings of texts, anthems for special occasions and services, additional Anglican chants, and several simplified Anglican chant formulas.

Q QUESTIONS FOR REFLECTION
AND DISCUSSION

1. Open the front of *The Hymnal 1982* and examine the service music table of contents. How is the layout similar to the 1979 Book of Common Prayer? How is it different? Is there any terminology you do not understand?

2. Glance through the first portion of service music: S1 to S66. If you are familiar with the Morning and Evening Prayer liturgies in the Book of Common Prayer, the texts should look familiar. Does your church regularly sing these portions of the liturgy? If so, do they use the Rite I or Rite II versions?

3. The Book of Common Prayer also lists sections devoted to collects, pastoral offices, episcopal services, and prayers and thanksgivings. Why are there no sections of *The Hymnal 1982* devoted to these texts? Should there be?

4. Read through the fourteen canticles in the Rite II section of the Book of Common Prayer. Which ones speak to you, and why? Have you ever experienced the apocryphal texts before? If so, how, when, and where?

The Hymnal 1982: Hymns

> Be filled with the Spirit, as you sing psalms and hymns and spiritual songs among yourselves, singing and making melody to the Lord in your hearts, giving thanks to God the Father at all times and for everything in the name of our Lord Jesus Christ.
>
> *Ephesians 5:18–20*

To many parishioners, hymns are the ultimate expression of corporate worship. There is also a sentimental aspect to the hymn literature. Most of us would have difficulty responding to the question, "What is your favorite service music setting?" However, most Episcopalians—from the sporadic worshipper to the faithful parishioner who attends every Sunday of the year—have a short (or long) list of favorite hymns.

Hymn singing has a rich and long tradition. In fact, many of the hymns in *The Hymnal 1982* were also a part of *The Hymnal 1940*. Some have been perennial favorites for centuries. Perhaps most important, hymns enrich our worship. Martin Luther is said to have held up a Bible in one hand, saying, "This is the Word of God," and a hymnal in the other, continuing, "and this is how we remember it." While this legend cannot be proven, it points to the power of hymn singing in worship.

WHAT IS A HYMN?

Although the exact origins of the term "hymn" are unknown, we know that the ancient Greeks and Romans used it to designate a poem in honor of a god. The early Christians adopted the word to designate hymns of praise to God that were distinct from the Psalms. Hymns may be poetic renderings of biblical passages or a newly composed religious text. From the earliest days, these songs of praise were gathered together in hymn collections or books. While hymns are generally sung, the word "hymn" technically only refers to the text. Most people, however, use the term more broadly. When thinking of a certain hymn, the tune (or tunes) most often associated with that text also comes to mind.

A BRIEF HISTORY OF ANGLICAN HYMNODY

The history of Anglican hymnody is a topic that is worthy of a book; it is far too complex to be condensed into several paragraphs. A few general comments, however, can be helpful in understanding the origins of the nineteenth-century English hymn and its influence on *The Hymnal 1982.*

The Bohemian Brethren compiled the earliest recorded hymnbook in 1505. Shortly thereafter, the early Lutheran Church developed the practice of singing chorales, a distinctly Lutheran hymn sung in the German vernacular. These chorales have had significant influence on early Protestant hymnody, and many of their tunes are included in contemporary hymnals, including *The Hymnal 1982.* When hymn tunes have a German name, chances are they are a product of this Lutheran tradition.

In an early draft of the Book of Common Prayer, Thomas Cranmer included twenty-six Latin hymns for use in the daily offices, but these were ultimately omitted when the all-English prayer book was published in 1549. This absence of hymnody became a hallmark of the early Church of England. In fact, for most of the Anglican Church's history, hymn singing was not permitted in cathedrals. Nevertheless, by the eighteenth century congregational hymn singing began occurring with regularity in smaller parishes, particularly those without the resources to provide choirs and organs. Without choir or organ, there could be no "professional" musical offerings made; perhaps more significant, the influences of the Puritan and Reformation traditions encouraged greater congregational participation over any "Popish" vestige of professional music-making in worship.

At the turn of the eighteenth century, Isaac Watts emerged as an important English hymn writer. His principle was that the texts should reflect the thoughts and feelings of those singing the texts. Watts even adapted the psalms in this way, which was quite radical for the time. His most important collection was *Hymns and Spiritual Songs* (1707), at the time the most complete collection of English hymnody ever produced. A glance in the index of *The Hymnal 1982* reveals seventeen hymn texts written by Watts. Other important hymn writers began to emerge shortly after Watts, the most important of whom were Charles Wesley and John Mason Neale.

In 1820, the hymnwriter and poet James Montgomery was placed on trial for writing hymns intended for public worship. His case was dismissed by the Archbishop of York. The "York Decision" (as it came to be known) effectively established the legality of the use of hymns in the Anglican liturgy and resulted in an explosion of new Anglican hymn tunes over the course of the nineteenth century. In 1861, the first edition of *Hymns Ancient and Modern* was published. This volume became the most important hymnal of the nineteenth century, undergoing many revisions and reissues over the course of the next fifty years. *Hymns Ancient and Modern* had considerable influence on the 1916 Episcopal hymnal as well as *The Hymnal 1940*.

The history of hymnology is a fascinating topic. For a more through history of British and American hymnody, the essays in *A Historical Survey of Christian Hymnody in the United States and Britain* (included in the first volume of *The Hymnal 1982 Companion,* edited by Raymond F. Glover) are an excellent resource.

COMPONENTS OF A HYMN
Texts (the Hymn Itself)
Unlike service music, hymns texts are not found in the Book of Common Prayer. Hymns are usually written in a specific poetic meter; they often have rhyme schemes, and they are strophic in nature, meaning that there are usually multiple stanzas (or verses). These poetic elements of hymns are important, as they lend themselves particularly well to musical settings.

Meters
The meter of a hymn refers to the syllabic layout of its text. In *The Hymnal 1982,* the meter is the number or abbreviation that appears on the lower right-hand corner of the page (or the last page of the hymn in the case of multiple pages). This number or abbreviation tells the reader exactly how many syllables are in each line of a stanza of the hymn. Different numbers (for each line) are separated by periods. For example, 11.11.11.5 indicates that there are four lines; the first three lines each have eleven syllables, and there are five syllables in the last line. There are several meters, or patterns of syllables per line of poetry, found in *The Hymnal 1982*; some appear regularly.

◆ CM (Common Meter = 8.6.8.6): The name is appropriate, as this is probably the most frequently encountered meter in all of hymnody. Common meter hymns are set in quatrains alternating between lines of eight and six syllables. In common meter, the second and fourth lines almost always rhyme, and the first and third lines sometimes do. "Amazing Grace" (NEW BRITAIN, 671) is one of the many examples of common meter in *The Hymnal 1982*. A fun bit of trivia: much of the poetry of Emily Dickinson is written in common meter, perhaps in homage to the strictly religious environment in which she lived.

♦ LM (Long Meter = 8.8.8.8): Long meter indicates eight syllables per line. The rhyme scheme can be either *abab* (as in common meter) or *aabb*. "O Wondrous Type! O Vision Fair" (WAREHAM, 137) and "All Praise to Thee, My God, This Night" (THE EIGHTH TUNE, 43) are both examples of long meter.

♦ SM (Short Meter = 6.6.8.6): Short meter indicates six syllables in each line with the exception of the third, which has eight. Like common meter, the second and fourth lines always rhyme. The first and third lines often do as well. "Praise We the Lord This Day" (ST. GEORGE, 267) is an example of short meter.

♦ D (Doubled): The letter "D" after a meter means "doubled"; standard meter patterns are often doubled in longer hymns. For example, "O Jesus, Crowned with All Renown" (KINGSFOLD, 292) has the meter labeled CMD, which means "common meter doubled" (8.6.8.6.8.6.8.6).

Not all hymn meters fall into standardized patterns, but this system allows any meter to be coded and catalogued. The most unusual meters in *The Hymnal 1982* usually apply to those hymns based on plainchant. For example, "Dost Thou in a Manger Lie" (DIES EST LAETITIAE, 97) has a meter that is notated as "76.76.775.775." This indicates four phrases (of 13, 13, 19, and 19 syllables, respectively) with each phrase divided into subphrases (two subphrases in the first two and three in the last two). Although these unusual meters may seem to lack a pattern altogether, *The Hymnal 1982* nevertheless includes a metrical number for each hymn regardless of the musical style or origin. Irregular meters (ones that do not fit into a regular pattern of syllables) are sometimes simply marked as such, with the abbreviation "Irr." "Were You There When They Crucified My Lord?" (WERE YOU THERE, 172) is one such example.

Occasionally, hymns also have refrains, a phrase or two that is sung after each stanza of the hymn. Generally, refrains will use the same text each time they are sung, whereas stanzas of a hymn are set to different poetic stanzas. To indicate refrains in metric notation, the word "refrain" is simply included after the numbers. The meter for "Angels We Have Heard on High" (GLORIA, 96), for instance, is labeled "77.77 with Refrain."

Hymn meter does not discriminate between accented syllables and less important syllables. It is up to the composer to stress the important syllables through their musical setting. Usually, more important syllables are set on longer and higher notes. A well-constructed hymn tune will follow the natural rise and fall of the declamatory line of the hymn.

Hymn texts that share a meter can be interchanged with alternate tunes of the same meter. For instance, "There Is a Green Hill Far Away," "Amazing Grace," and "O, for a Thousand Tongues to Sing" are all common meter hymns and may be sung to HORSLEY, NEW BRITAIN, or AZMON interchangeably and more or less successfully. The key (major or minor), tempo, and pairing of emphasized musical beats to emphasized syllables must also be considered when making a pairing of tune and text.

Tunes
The tune is the melody of the hymn. Hymn tunes have many sources. Many are composed by individuals, whereas others are folk songs or are so old that the composer has been forgotten. When the composer cannot be identified with cer-

tainty, the source of the hymn tune is listed at the bottom of the page.

Each hymn tune has its own distinct name. While slight variations can occur between hymnals of different denominations, a hymn tune is an interdenominational code that can only refer to one melody. As noted earlier, in *The Hymnal 1982* the name of the hymn tune is listed in italics (*Hyfrydol, Easter Hymn*), but all-capital letters (HYFRYDOL, EASTER HYMN) are used in this book to eliminate confusion between other italicized titles, such as book titles, major works, and terminology from foreign languages.

Hymn tunes can appear in any key. Changing the key of a tune does not change the name of the tune, though a change of mode—from major to minor or vice versa—can result in a change of the hymn tune name.[14] When compiling hymnals, editors generally place hymns in a range that is neither too high nor too low. Good hymn keys are ones that are friendly to untrained voices and suitable for congregational singing.

Harmonizations

Most hymns are written in four-part harmony, with the top line (soprano) singing the hymn tune. The other three parts are called—from highest to lowest—the alto, tenor, and bass. The soprano and alto are written in the upper of the two staves (entitled a "grand staff") with the tenor and bass written in the lower one. The soprano and tenor "stems" of the notes point upward, and the alto and bass stems point downward; this allows the singer to follow his or her part with greater clarity.

Sometimes, hymns are not written in four parts; only the tune is included. In these hymns, everyone is expected to sing the melody. Although many hymns can be sung *a cappella* (without accompaniment), organ accompaniments are provided for all of the hymns in *The Hymnal 1982*. Often, congregations experiment with singing the interior stanzas of a more contemplative hymn *a cappella*. Unaccompanied singing is particularly effective (and more historically accurate) in plainchant genres.

Descants
As mentioned in chapter 2, descants are alternate melodic lines composed to sound above the hymn tune. When performed, descants are then heard as the highest voice, adding excitement and contrast to the final stanzas of hymns. Descants are included in *The Hymnal 1982* for a number of hymns.

Asterisks
Asterisks (*) appear frequently throughout the hymnal in front of selected stanzas of hymns. They indicate stanzas that can be omitted without compromising the integrity of the text or the theological message behind the hymn. For example, "Not Here for High and Holy Things" (MORNING SONG, 9) has asterisks listed before the first three stanzas; this means that the hymn may be sung using stanzas 4 through 6 only. If an asterisk does not appear, then the hymn should be sung in its entirety; omissions are not encouraged.

If a hymn has five or more stanzas, a small horizontal line will appear separating stanzas 3 and 4. Appearing consistently along the left-hand margin of the page (below the clefs), these lines simply help the reader of hymns guide his or her eyes quickly to the appropriate stanza. This line is *not* the same as an asterisk, and stanzas that occur below this line should not be omitted from services.

HYMN SELECTION
The Book of Common Prayer says very little about music in general, and is almost equally silent on hymnody. By and large, hymns are determined entirely at the discretion of the rector, often with input from the choirmaster and organist. The Book of Common Prayer mentions specific hymns on only three occasions: "All Glory, Laud, and Honor" on Palm Sunday (BCP 271); "Sing, My Tongue, the Glorious Battle" on Good

Friday (BCP 282); and either VENI CREATOR SPIRITUS (502 or 504) or VENI SANCTE SPIRITUS (226) at ordinations (BCP 520, 533, and 544). No other specific hymns are mentioned or prescribed.

Hymns are selected in consultation with the *Revised Common Lectionary,* the prescribed three-year rotation of scripture readings used by the Episcopal Church and most other liturgically centered denominations. The *Revised Common Lectionary* mirrors the church year, beginning each year on the first Sunday of Advent and concluding with Proper 29, sometimes known as the Reign of Christ or Christ the King Sunday. Readings consist of passages from both the Old and New Testaments, a Psalm, and a Gospel. Year A centers around the Gospel of Matthew, Year B around Mark, and Year C around Luke. Readings from the Gospel of John may be found throughout all three years. Well-selected hymns will amplify the lessons for that particular Sunday.

HYMN CATEGORIZATION
The hymns included in *The Hymnal 1982* are categorized according to the daily office and the church year; the sacraments of Holy Baptism, the Holy Eucharist, confirmation, and marriage; burials, ordinations, and the consecration of a church. There is also a large section for general hymns (ones that do not fit neatly into any specific category). Additional information on hymn texts may be found in Nancy Roth's three books of hymn-based meditations: *A Closer Walk* (1998), *Awake My Soul!* (1999), and *New Every Morning* (2000), as well as Raymond Glover's four-volume *The Hymnal 1982 Companion* (1990).

THE DAILY OFFICE (1–46)
The first forty-six hymns in *The Hymnal 1982* are devoted to the daily office. Although the service music section of the hymnal only included music for the two principal offices—Morning and Evening Prayer—the hymn section includes options for the Noonday and Compline liturgies as well.

Daily Morning Prayer (1–11)
Most of the hymns offered for Morning Prayer are simple in
nature, offering a single melodic line in praise of God; only
Hymn 7 (RATISBON), Hymn 8 (BUNESSAN), and Hymn 11
(MORNING HYMN) are written in four-part harmony. Hymns
9 (MORNING SONG) and 10 (KEDRON) both offer asterisks
on three of their six stanzas; this truncation allows for the option of more concise hymn-singing during Morning Prayer.

Noonday (12–23)
The twelve hymns of Noonday are similar to those of Morning
Prayer in their simplicity. Again, only three hymns are harmonized: Hymn 20 (WAREHAM), Hymn 21 (SONG 34), and
Hymn 23 (DU MEINER SEELEN). Gregorian plainchant settings also proliferate, perhaps alluding to the ancient origins
of noonday prayer; these plainchant settings include Hymns
13, 15, 16, 18, 19, and 22.

An Order of Worship for the Evening
and Daily Evening Prayer (24–37)
Fourteen hymns for Evening Prayer are included in *The Hymnal 1982*. Included are two settings of the hymn tune BROM-
LEY (Hymns 28 and 29). "O Gladsome Light" (Hymn 36)
and the round "O Gracious Light" (Hymn 25) are both paraphrases of the *Phos hilaron,* an ancient Greek Christian hymn
associated with Evening Prayer.

Compline (38–46)
Like An Order of Service for Noonday, the office of Compline
is not prayed in community with the same frequency as Morning or Evening Prayer. The nine hymns include a Lutheran
chorale (Hymn 46), a round (Hymn 43), and three Gregorian
plainchant settings. David Hurd also contributes a contemporary plainchant setting (COMPLINE, 41).

THE CHURCH YEAR (47–293)

Just as the seasons of the church year inform the liturgy as it is outlined in the Book of Common Prayer, *The Hymnal 1982* is also organized in part according to the church year. Hymns specifically appropriate for Advent through the Day of Pentecost are represented in this section of the hymnal. During the rest of the church year—Trinity Sunday through Proper 29, also known as The Reign of Christ or Christ the King Sunday—hymns are generally selected from other sections of *The Hymnal 1982*, particularly the vast "General Hymns" section (362–634), paying attention to the lessons assigned to that day.

Sunday (47–52)

Sunday is obviously not a season, but hymns that directly reference the day are a welcome part of any Sunday Eucharist. Out of these six hymns, "We the Lord's People" (DECATUR PLACE, 51) is probably the most well-known.

Advent (53–76)

The season of Advent, the first season of the church year, begins four Sundays before Christmas. It is a season of preparation for the birth of Jesus and the second coming of Christ, and a sense of anticipation is heard in many of these twenty-four selections.

Christmas (77–115)

Perhaps no section of *The Hymnal 1982* is as familiar as the Christmas portion, which contains some of the most enduring carols, melodies, and words of the season. Indeed, many of these hymns are found in hymnals of every Christian denomination, though there may be slight variation in terms of text, melody, and harmony.

Blended with these familiar favorites are several that are less well-known, as well as some twentieth-century hymns by living composers. Particularly beautiful is "A Stable Lamp Is Lighted" (ANDÚJAR, 104) by David Hurd.

Epiphany (116–139)

The Feast of the Epiphany is celebrated on January 6, twelve days after the birth of Christ, and the season after the Epiphany lasts until Ash Wednesday, which begins Lent. Depending on when Easter falls, the season after the Epiphany may be from four to eight weeks. While most Epiphany hymns have not achieved widespread appeal, the exception to this rule is "We Three Kings of Orient Are" (THREE KINGS OF ORIENT, 128), which has become popular across denominations; it is perhaps the only "famous" Epiphany hymn.

It should be mentioned that the order of hymns within any given section of the hymnal does not necessarily correlate with when in the season particular hymns should be sung. In other words, hymns at the end of a section are not necessarily sung at the end of a season. Hymns 122 (URBS BEATA JERUSALEM) and 123 (TIBI CHRISTE, SPLENDOR PATRIS), for example, are clearly hymns for the last Sunday after the Epiphany, even though they fall toward the beginning of *The Hymnal 1982*'s selection of Epiphany hymns.

Lent (140–152)

These hymns evoke the penitential spirit of Lent. Like the weeks after Epiphany, the five-Sunday season of Lent also offers challenges to congregations who use *The Hymnal 1982*, as only thirteen hymns comprise this section of the hymnal. The relative brevity of this section assumes that hymns relevant to the Propers of each Sunday in Lent will be drawn from other sections of the hymnal.

Holy Week (153–173)

Holy Week begins with Palm Sunday. This section of the hymnal opens, unusually, not with a hymn but rather with plainchant settings (153) to be used during the Liturgy of the Palms (BCP 270–272). "All Glory, Laud, and Honor"—one of the only hymns specifically recommended by the Book of Common Prayer—is then set to two different tunes as Hymns 154 and 155. The rest of the hymns provided may be used at various times during Holy Week. Churches are generally silent on Holy Saturday until the evening, when the Easter Vigil is held.

Easter (174–213)

Easter, the celebration of the resurrection of Christ from the dead, is the most important of all Christian celebrations. Easter Day may be a single occasion, but the Easter season lasts for seven weeks (and eight Sundays). *The Hymnal 1982* includes forty hymns for this season. While all of them may be sung throughout the Easter season, two are particularly important to Easter Day itself. "Jesus Christ Is Risen Today" (EASTER HYMN, 207) is the quintessential Easter morning hymn, often accompanied by brass fanfares in celebration of the resurrection. Easter Day also usually marks the appearance of "Hail Thee, Festival Day!" (SALVE FESTA DIES, 175). The Easter version of this hymn has eight stanzas, and it is often used as an elaborate processional or recessional; this hymn is also generally sung on Ascension and Pentecost with alternate words (see Hymns 216 and 225). Descants on final stanzas of hymns are particularly appropriate and frequently heard on Easter Day and throughout the Easter season.

Ascension Day (214–222)

Ascension Day commemorates the bodily ascension of Jesus into heaven. Occurring on the fortieth day after Easter, it always falls on a Thursday, and many churches hold special services to celebrate Ascension Day. Like Easter and Pentecost, "Hail Thee, Festival Day!" (SALVE FESTA DIES, 216) is usually sung in its six-stanza version to an Ascension Day text.

The Day of Pentecost (223–230)

The Day of Pentecost marks the end of the Easter season. "Hail Thee, Festival Day!" (SALVE FESTA DIES, 225)—also sung at Easter (175) and Ascension (216)—makes its third and final appearance in this section. With only four stanzas, it is the shortest of the three appearances of this hymn. Also particularly interesting is a metric setting of VENI SANCTE SPIRITUS (226). "Hail This Joyful Day's Return" (223) is also the only appearance in the entire hymnal of the plainchant hymn tune BEATA NOBIS GAUDIA.

Holy Days, the Common of Saints, and Various Occasions (231–293)

This healthy collection of sixty-three hymns is intended for use on feast days commemorating saints. "By All Your Saints Still Striving" (KING'S LYNN, 231 and NYLAND, 232) are particularly interesting, offering up twelve choices for the interior stanzas of each of these hymns. While the first and third stanzas are sung to the same text each time, the second stanza varies depending on the saint honored. A list of saints with their respective stanzas is printed on the pages facing the hymns. This section of the hymnal concludes with some hymns that generally praise all the saints. The two most famous are "For All the Saints" (SINE NOMINE, 287) by Ralph Vaughan Williams and "I Sing a Song of the Saints of God" (GRAND ISLE, 293) by John Henry Hopkins. Perhaps no other hymns in the entire hymnal are as unapologetically Anglican as these two selections.

HOLY BAPTISM (294–299)

It is perhaps surprising that there are only six hymns in *The Hymnal 1982* specifically devoted to baptism, given its significance to the ecclesiology of the 1979 Book of Common Prayer. The most famous may be "We Know That Christ Is Raised and Dies No More" (ENGELBERG, 296), whose tune is composed by Charles Villiers Stanford, one of the most important of all Anglican composers. "Baptized in Water, Sealed by the Spirit" (POINT LOMA, 294) is a contemporary text to a tune by David Charles Walker.

THE HOLY EUCHARIST (300–347)

The sacrament of the Holy Eucharist is well-represented in *The Hymnal 1982*. Most of these hymns are contemplative in nature and may be sung as the people are receiving communion. Although it specifically references the Eucharist, "Lord, Enthroned in Heavenly Splendor" (BRYN CALFARIA, 307) works as an excellent recessional hymn at the end of a service.

CONFIRMATION (348–349)

The two hymns recognizing the sacramental action of confirmation are "Lord, We Have Come at Your Own Invitation" (O QUANTA QUALIA, 348) and "Holy Spirit, Lord of Love" (ABERYSTWYTH, 349). The latter is a chorale-like tune in four-part harmony, the former a unison melody.

MARRIAGE (350–353)

Perhaps surprisingly, only four hymns are included regarding marriage. This very interesting short section of the hymnal offers a variety of tunes, one from each of the four most recent centuries: the seventeenth (CAITHNESS, 352), eighteenth (HALTON HOLGATE, 351), nineteenth (WAREHAM, 353), and twentieth (ST. MARY MAGDALENE, 350).

BURIAL OF THE DEAD (354–358)

In these three hymns, the gravity of death is musically represented through plainchant (IN PARADISUM, 354) and with a Lutheran chorale tune (CHRISTUS, DER IST MEIN LEBEN, 356). "Give Rest, O Christ, to Your Servants with Your Saints" (KONTAKION, 355) is a very interesting selection as it is the only hymn in the entire hymnal that is based upon an Eastern Orthodox Slavonic chant.

ORDINATION (359)

The five-stanza "God of the Prophets" (TOULON, 359) is the only hymn in *The Hymnal 1982* specifically categorized as an ordination hymn. The original third stanza was based on a theology of ordination that did not give sufficient attention to the importance of baptism, and was therefore revised by Carl P. Daw, Jr., for *The Hymnal 1982*:

> Anoint them priests! help them to intercede
> with all thy royal priesthood born of grace;
> through them thy Church presents in word and deed
> Christ's one true sacrifice with thankful praise.

The other four stanzas comprised the original hymn, which was written by Denis Wortman.

CONSECRATION OF A CHURCH (360–361)
These two hymns both have six stanzas set to one monophonic (single melodic) line. ROUEN (360) is a seventeenth-century hymn tune, whereas CAELITUM JOSEPH (361) is Gregorian plainsong chant.

GENERAL HYMNS (362–634)
By far the largest section of *The Hymnal 1982*, general hymns can be used in multiple ways and on a variety of occasions.

The Holy Trinity (362–371)
The Holy Trinity is the Christian doctrine that defines God as three consubstantial persons: the Father, the Son (Jesus Christ), and the Holy Spirit (or Holy Ghost). These ten hymns specifically reference the Trinity and dovetail beautifully with the many passages of scripture that reference the Holy Trinity in the lectionary.

Praise to God (372–433)
Like the Psalms, these fifty-two hymns are expressions of praise to God. In this sense, many could also be labeled as "doxologies" ("short hymns of praise to God"). The tune OLD 100TH appears three times (setting three different texts) in this section: Hymns 377, 378, and 380. "Joyful, Joyful, We Adore Thee" (HYMN TO JOY, 376) is an adaptation of the famous

chorus from the last movement of the ninth symphony of
Ludwig von Beethoven.

Jesus Christ Our Lord (434–499)

This generous sampling of sixty-six hymns directly reference
Jesus.

The Holy Spirit (500–516)

The seventeen hymns in this section directly mention the
Holy Spirit. "Come, Holy Ghost" (COME HOLY GHOST, 503)
is a particularly interesting inclusion, as it is the only selection
in *The Hymnal 1982* for soloist (cantor) and congregation.

The Church (517–527)

In this section are eleven general hymns to the church. The
most well-known may be "Christ Has Made the Sure Foundation" (WESTMINSTER ABBEY, 518) and "I Love Thy Kingdom, Lord" (ST. THOMAS [WILLIAMS], 524).

The Church's Mission (528–544)

Evangelism, or at least the Episcopal version of it, permeates
these seventeen hymns. Each speaks of the Great Commission
in some way or another, reminding us to "go therefore and
make disciples of all nations" (Matthew 28:19).

Christian Vocation and Pilgrimage (545–565)

These twenty-one hymns speak directly of the "journey" or
"pilgrimage" experience of the Christian. Many of the hymns
in this collection also have a certain pietistic quality, both in
their words and music. Some of the most recognizable of these
include "Rejoice, Ye Pure in Heart!" (MARION, 556), "Faith
of Our Fathers!" (ST. CATHERINE, 558), "Stand Up, Stand Up,
for Jesus" (MORNING LIGHT, 561), and "Onward, Christian
Soldiers" (ST. GERTRUDE, 562). Another interesting inclusion
is "'Tis the Gift to Be Simple" (SIMPLE GIFTS, 554), a Shaker
tune made famous through the Pulitzer Prize–winning ballet

Appalachian Spring (1944) by the American composer Aaron Copland.

Christian Responsibility (566–612)

This extensive collection of forty-seven hymns is sadly neglected in many Episcopal parishes. JERUSALEM (597), a hymn tune written by Charles Hubert Hastings Parry in 1916, is a composition entwined with the very identity of England; it appears here, however, paired with a contemporary text by Carl P. Daw, Jr., instead of the instantly recognizable early nineteenth-century English political poem by William Blake.

The Kingdom of God (613–617)

This short section of five hymns has texts that allude to the kingdom of God. They are excellent choices for communion and are frequently sung at that spot during the service.

The Church Triumphant (618–625)

This is a grouping of eight hymns whose texts are particularly exultant in nature. The most famous tunes in this section are LASST UNS ERFREUEN (618)—set to the text "Ye Watchers and Ye Holy Ones"—and LAND OF REST ("Jerusalem, My Happy Home," 620).

Holy Scripture (626–634)

While many hymns reference scripture, these are hymns that speak directly to the importance of God's word in our daily life. Hymn 626 (QUAM DILECTA) begins with the words, "Lord, be thy word my rule; in it may I rejoice," and Hymn 628 (ST. ETHELWALD) begins, "Help us, O Lord, to learn the truths your word imparts." Hymn 631, "Book of Books, Our People's Strength" (LIEBSTER JESU), devotes three stanzas entirely to the Bible. Written by Percy Dearmer, the second stanza is particularly memorable:

Thank we those who toiled in thought,
   many diverse scrolls completing,
poets, prophets, scholars, saints,
   each a word from God repeating;
till they came, who told the story
   of the Word, and showed his glory.

THE CHRISTIAN LIFE (635–709)

This extensive section of *The Hymnal 1982* groups together seventy-five hymns. In some ways, this is the most diverse section of the hymnal; "When Israel Was in Egypt's Land" (GO DOWN, MOSES, 648) takes its place alongside "O Jesus, Joy of Loving Hearts" (DICKINSON COLLEGE, 649). All are loosely grouped under the broad theme of "the Christian life." On a practical level, these are simply hymns that do not fit neatly into the other categories established in *The Hymnal 1982*. Nevertheless, this section of the hymnal contains some of the Episcopal Church's most beloved and enduring hymns, including "The King of Love My Shepherd Is" (ST. COLUMBA, 645), "How Firm a Foundation" (FOUNDATION, 636 and LYONS, 637), "Dear Lord and Father of Mankind" (REPTON, 653), "Day by Day" (SUMNER, 654), and "Love Divine, All Loves Excelling" (HYFRYDOL, 657), and "O God, Our Help in Ages Past (ST. ANNE, 680).

ROUNDS AND CANONS (710–715)

This short section of six hymns gathers together half a dozen rounds and canons. While several are traditional, including DONA NOBIS PACEM (712) and SHALOM CHAVERIM (714), SEEK YE FIRST (711) is a twentieth-century composition in the popular/folk style by Karen Lafferty.

NATIONAL SONGS (716–720)

The hymn tune AMERICA is used on two distinct texts: "God Bless Our Native Land" (716) and the more familiar "My Country 'Tis of Thee" (717). The other three are equally well-known: "God of Our Fathers" (NATIONAL HYMN, 718), "America" (MATERNA, 719), and "The Star-Spangled Banner" (NATIONAL ANTHEM, 720). Although the practice is liturgically questionable, many parishes incorporate these hymns on Sundays coinciding with national holidays such as Independence Day, Flag Day, or on Memorial Day weekend. They may also be used when churches host civic events.

INDICES TO *THE HYMNAL 1982*

The Hymnal 1982 has a variety of indices. The copyright acknowledgments section (which is technically not an index) is self-explanatory: these are the "permissions" acquired so that material, under copyright with other publishers, could be legally reprinted. The next four indices allow the user of *The Hymnal 1982* to look up hymns in four different ways: by author, translator, or source (of the hymn text); by composer, arranger, or source (of the hymn tune); by the hymn tune name; and by the first line of the hymn (which is usually not the same as the hymn tune name).

It is curious that *The Hymnal 1982* does not include a metrical index in the standard pew edition. These indices—which appear in many hymnals—allow the choirmaster to mix and match tunes with texts that share the same meter. A metrical index is included, however, in the accompaniment edition of *The Hymnal 1982,* as well as *The Hymnbook 1982* (an ecumenical edition of the hymnal).

Q QUESTIONS FOR REFLECTION AND DISCUSSION

1. Hymns often have deep spiritual meaning to people. If attending church was part of your upbringing, think of your favorite hymns from childhood. Which ones were they? If you grew up with *The Hymnal 1940* or in another denomination, are your favorites still included in *The Hymnal 1982*? (Use the index to look up both the first line and the tune, if you happen

to know it. Sometimes texts can appear with different tunes, and tunes with different words.)

2. The next time you sing a hymn in church, take in all of the details on the page. In what section of the hymnal does this hymn reside? Who wrote the text (or from where does it come)? What is the tune name, and who wrote it (or from where does it come)? Why do you think this hymn was chosen for this particular Sunday? (Hint: How does it relate to the season or Gospel reading?)

3. Find two hymns in *The Hymnal 1982* that have the same meter. Ideally, try to pick two hymns with which you are very familiar or that you have committed to memory. In your mind, "switch" the tunes and sing the each text to the "opposite" hymn tune. (It should be possible.) What is your reaction? Do you find it refreshing, interesting, strange, or unwelcome?

4. What is your favorite season of the church year? Do the hymns sung during that season have anything to do with your preference?

The Choir and
Its Offerings

Sing praises to God, sing praises; *
   sing praises to our King, sing praises.
For God is King of all the earth; *
   sing praises with all your skill.

Psalm 47:6–7 (BCP 650)

The choir fills an important role in the Episcopal Church. Throughout most of the history of the Church of England, choirs were elite ensembles that, along with the organist, carried the musical portions of the liturgy. Congregations in cathedrals would sit politely in the pews and listen to full "choral Eucharists" that were executed entirely by the choir. Hymns were not even permitted to be sung in the Church of England until the York Decision of 1820. Since that time, hymnody has occupied a more substantial role, but the cathedral culture—which prioritizes the tradition of choral excellence—is still valued, particularly during the Eucharist and at Evensong. Generally speaking, the more "high church" an atmosphere, the more choral offerings will comprise the service. From a musical perspective, "low church" is more congregational, "high church" more choral.

Congregational singing has been an important part of the Episcopal Church since its very beginning. While some parishes—usually in major metropolitan areas—can maintain full choral Eucharists or daily Evensong, the vast majority could not afford to do so even if they wanted to. Perhaps more important, most Episcopal churches value congregational participation in the music-making. In these parishes, the principal role of the choir is to provide musical leadership for the congregation.

HYMN AND SERVICE MUSIC LEADERSHIP

Occasionally, Episcopal Church choirs are comprised completely of professional singers. This occurs only in a small percentage of parishes, usually in endowed churches in major metropolitan eras. The majority of Episcopal Church choirs are comprised primarily of volunteers. In these churches, the choir can be thought of as a ministry similar to the altar guild, flower guild, or outreach committee. Most choirs have weekly rehearsals with extra rehearsals sometimes called for special musical events such as Lessons and Carols or major works. Choirs may prepare an anthem every Sunday of the church year, in addition to Evensong and other services and events. Consistent attendance is essential, as missing too many rehearsals can be detrimental to the choir and its preparation; this is why many choirmasters have strict attendance policies. For all of these reasons, the choir is perhaps the most time-consuming ministry in the church, but it is also one of the most fulfilling.

In addition to the offering of an anthem, the principal role of the choir is to lead the people in musical worship. Less musically confident members of the congregation tend to "lean on" the leadership of the choir when singing hymns and service music. Most choirmasters will ask the choir to sing in unison (on the hymn melody) during the first stanzas of hymns to help lead the congregation. Harmonies are explored on interior stanzas as the congregation gains confidence. Unlike the choir, the majority of parishioners will likely sing the melody for all stanzas.

Occasionally, a hymn will be chosen that is less familiar to the congregation. When this occurs, the choir plays a significant role in introducing the hymn to the congregation. As most hymns consist of multiple stanzas, congregations will generally sing more robustly as the hymn progresses and the tune becomes more familiar. Changes in the church season may also coincide with rotations of the service music, and the choir (which has been rehearsing and is alert to the changes) plays an important role in managing the seasonal transitions smoothly.

WHAT IS UNIQUE ABOUT AN EPISCOPAL CHOIR?

Choral music is one of the Episcopal Church's proudest customs, and over the centuries a rich and varied body of repertoire has been composed for choirs in the Anglican tradition. This tradition is unique in that throughout most of its history, Anglican choirs were comprised of men and boys. This all-male sound made for a particularly homogenous and seamless texture. The roster of King's College, Cambridge still maintains a choir of thirty male singers, which includes sixteen trebles (boys with unchanged voices), six altos (male falsettists), four tenors, and four basses.

During the second half of the nineteenth century, choir manuals were written for the first time. The primary purpose of these manuals was to help choirmasters in smaller parishes cultivate and build a choral culture. The modern sound of the Anglican choir may have been codified during this time. Words like "fluty," "ethereal," "impersonal," and—especially—"discipline" exemplify the Anglican ideal. Perhaps no choral style demands more from voices in terms of discipline and restraint. While some choral styles permit vibrato (African-American spirituals come to mind), most choirmasters would agree that a certain amount of straight-tone singing is an absolute must in Anglican styles.

While some Episcopal churches continue the all-male Anglican tradition, the vast majority of Episcopal choirs have become mixed ensembles, incorporating women into their ranks. Although most choirmasters still strive to achieve an ideal Anglican choral aesthetic when rehearsing and performing Anglican repertoire, mixed choirs ultimately sound a bit different from all-male ensembles. In spite of these challenges, most mixed choirs have risen to the challenge, and many of the best Episcopal church choirs in the country include women on their rosters.

A NOTE ON CHURCH ARCHITECTURE

Before proceeding further, a brief note must be made concerning church architecture, as it bears considerable significance on the repertoire composed for Anglican choirs over the course of its long history. In the English tradition, most cathedrals placed their choirs on either side of the front chancel area. The altar usually occupied the eastern end of the cathedral, with the two chancel areas positioned to the north and south. The north chancel was called the "cantoris," which literally means "of the cantor"; it was the side of the chancel area where the cantor—the historical equivalent of the modern choirmaster—resided. The south chancel was called the "decani," which literally means "of the dean"; it was the side of the chancel that the dean occupied. Thus, most of the music for the Anglican was written with this "split choir" formation in mind. Both "halves" of the choir were in effect their own individual choir, with all four parts represented on either side of the chancel. In addition to the anthems and service music that were specifically written for this "double choir" formation, the decani/cantoris designations become particularly important when rehearsing and performing Anglican chant psalmody, a genre that specifically designates that the two sides of the choir alternate verses antiphonally.

While the majority of Anglican and Episcopal choirs reside in the chancel area of the church, there are sometimes excep-

tions. The choir loft is perhaps the most frequently encountered alternative. Choir lofts are positioned in the back of the
nave and are usually elevated, accessible only by stairs or an
elevator. The organ console—and usually the organ
pipework—is also built in the same area of the church as the
choir: organ consoles will be in the loft in churches with choir
lofts and in the front in churches with chancel choirs.

ANTHEMS: A RICH REPERTOIRE

In the 1662 revision of the Book of Common Prayer, additional prayers were added to the end of Morning Prayer and
Evening Prayer. As a result, the service was lengthened, and a
new line was added to the liturgy that came to be known as
the "anthem rubric": "In quires and spires and places where
they sing, here followeth the anthem." This required and inspired new musical compositions to be inserted after the third
collect, and a new tradition was born. Composers began com-
posing anthems: settings of biblical or otherwise religious texts
appropriate for the liturgy. Composers, attracted to the creative opportunity of the genre—the texts selected were not
prescribed by the Book of Common Prayer but rather could
be chosen entirely at the discretion of the composer—began
to compose anthems prolifically. Over the course of the next
two hundred years, the anthem quickly became the Anglican
Church's most important musical genre.

In most Episcopal churches today, anthems are still heard
on a weekly basis during the Sunday Eucharist. While anthems
may be inserted in a variety of places, the most common spot
is the offertory. On a practical level, this placement is logical
as it provides music while the offering is being collected. The
ideal anthem—or any liturgical music for that matter—will
cover the length of time required for the corresponding liturgical activity. In larger parishes or more established music programs there may be two anthems, with the second anthem
generally occurring while the people are receiving communion. Anthems can occur at other moments in the service as

well. Morning and Evening Prayer also may include anthems as part of the liturgy.

Generally (but not always), anthems that set longer texts are also longer in length. As a result, anthem lengths can vary greatly. Gerald Finzi's "Lo, the Full Final Sacrifice" (1946) is sixteen minutes in length, whereas John Goss's "These Are They That Follow the Lamb" (1859) lasts only about a minute. Likewise, the difficulty of the anthem varies as well. Some choirs have the ability and size to perform virtually the entire anthem repertoire; these choirs can execute even the most difficult pieces with little trouble. Smaller churches with less developed or all-volunteer choirs generally choose anthems with fewer parts that are less difficult. The anthem repertoire contains enough variety to accommodate virtually every choir and liturgical situation, and choirmasters have a large repertoire of quality music from which to make their selections.

Biblical Texts and Translations

Many anthems are settings of passages from the Bible, which can fit well with the lessons (or readings) prescribed for the particular day by the *Revised Common Lectionary*. Choirmasters choose anthems very carefully to complement the lessons, particularly the Gospel. Texts for the anthems may be printed in the bulletin so that the congregation can follow along with the text and meditate on it. A well-chosen and well-sung anthem will amplify the Gospel, which has most likely also been expounded upon during the homily. The ideal is for both homily and anthem to complement and build upon the Gospel.

Although it is not at all a requirement, the text of the anthem is sometimes exactly the same as one of the lessons. This is actually a common occurrence, as most of the standard biblical lessons have been set by composers, both famous and lesser known, many times over the course of the history of church music. As a result, there are often several—even many—available choral settings of the same text. The decision of which one to program once again falls to the choirmaster, who will ultimately make the decision based on a variety of factors, and sometimes his or her own subjective opinion. Sometimes composers will splice together several biblical passages and conflate them into one anthem setting. One of Ralph Vaughan Williams's most famous anthems, "O How Amiable" (1934), is a classic example of this "mosaic" approach. In it, he combines texts from two different psalms, followed by a stanza of a well-known hymn. The anthem begins by setting verses 1–4 of Psalm 84 (Coverdale version):

> O how amiable are thy dwellings, thou Lord of hosts!
>   My soul hath a desire and longing to enter into
>   the courts of the Lord.
>   My heart and my flesh rejoice in the living God.

> Yea, the sparrow hath found her an house,
>   and the swallow a nest where she may lay her young;
>   even thy altars, O Lord of hosts, my King and my God.

> Blessed are they that dwell in thy house, they will be alway
>   praising thee.

After this, Vaughan Williams immediately incorporates the last verse of Psalm 90 (verse 17):

> The glorious Majesty of the Lord our God be upon us,
>   prosper thou the work of our hands upon us.
>   O prosper thou our handiwork.

Finally, to conclude the anthem, Vaughan Williams adds the first stanza of a familiar hymn by Isaac Watts. This hymn is included in *The Hymnal 1982* as Hymn 680 (ST. ANNE):

> O God, our help in ages past,
> our hope for years to come,
> our shelter from the stormy blast,
> and our eternal home.

An important note must also be made here regarding translations. As "O How Amiable" was written in 1934, the psalm translation that Vaughan Williams set is from the 1539 translation of the Psalms by Miles Coverdale, the same translation that appears in the 1928 Book of Common Prayer. American congregations may immediately notice that this translation of Psalms 84 and 90 is different from that in their 1979 Book of Common Prayer. This inconsistency between anthem texts and the other texts used in the service occurs regularly and presents no real problems to the liturgy.

Quite simply, it would be completely impractical—and a travesty—to forbid any of the wonderful psalm settings that were composed before 1979 or biblically based anthem texts set before 1989 (the year of the publication of the New Revised Standard Version of the Bible, the most commonly used Bible translation in the Episcopal Church). Not only would it eliminate the entire canon from the "golden era" of Anglican church music, but also any British composer of any era, as the 1979 Book of Common Prayer is only used in the Episcopal Church. In addition, it is also generally considered not to be feasible or appropriate to substitute or change words already set by a composer; this is actually illegal in works under copyright.

In short, most congregations and clergy understand the coexistence of multiple translations within a single service. Most contemporary Episcopal composers, a product of their time, will set texts in modern translation, and a wonderful new body of anthem repertoire and psalmody is emerging within the Episcopal Church.

WHY DO CHOIRS SOMETIMES SING IN FOREIGN LANGUAGES?

One of the primary ambitions behind the original Book of Common Prayer was to offer a distinctly English form of worship. Indeed, throughout most of the Anglican Church's history, services were executed entirely in the English vernacular.

Therefore, one could argue that programming sacred choral music in Latin, German, or another foreign language is the antithesis of the Anglican ideal and should be avoided at all costs.

This argument is certainly valid, but in the twenty-first century, reactions to foreign languages during the choral moments of a liturgy tend to be a little more relaxed. The Latin and German sacred choral repertoire is especially rich, offering gifts from Johann Sebastian Bach, Joseph Haydn, Wolfgang Amadeus Mozart, Johannes Brahms, and many others. Care is still taken, however, to ensure that the text being sung is appropriate within the particular liturgy. When selections are sung in a foreign language, an English translation should be printed in the bulletin for those who may be unfamiliar with the work or its text.

Just as choirs occasionally appropriate music originally written in foreign languages, it is also not unusual to hear sacred music from styles and genres that fall outside of the historical tradition of the Church of England. The African-American spiritual comes to mind as a genre that has found an ecumenical home across all denominations, including the Episcopal Church.

CHILDREN'S CHOIRS

In addition to the principal choir of the church, which is comprised primarily of adults, most Episcopal churches will also sponsor a children's choir program. Depending on the size of the church, children may begin singing as early as age five or six and continue until they reach high-school. Children's choirs are usually tiered according to age, sometimes singing at different services or times than the adult choir. A rich body of sacred choral music has been written for children's choirs, and certain festival anthems combine children with adult voices. Historically, many children's choirs were all-boys (especially in England), but in the United States most include both genders. Organizations like the Royal School of Church

Music (RSCM) and the Choristers Guild have been champions of children's choirs, sponsoring publications, conferences, workshops, and repertoire for children of all ages.

JOINING A CHURCH CHOIR

As an Episcopal choirmaster, I have the pleasure of meeting and greeting parishioners on a weekly basis during coffee hour, many of whom enjoy music very much. They often compliment me on the choir's sound or ask an insightful question about the anthem. And, sometimes (if I am very lucky), they ask a question that I love to hear: "I love singing in church, and am interested in singing in the choir. Can just anyone join the church choir?"

In my parish, the answer to this question is a resounding "yes!" Our music program depends almost entirely on volunteers. As long as someone is able to make a regular commitment to rehearsals and the Sunday liturgy, he or she is welcome to join the choir. But all churches (and choirs) are different. Large parishes or parishes with endowed music programs may require an audition process for prospective choristers. These auditions generally consist of singing a solo selection, sight reading, and a series of vocal exercises. Sometimes, even excellent singers with successful auditions are put on a waiting list until there is an opening in the choir, either due to issues of chancel area space or balance among the sections.

While auditions may not be required in most parishes, singing in a choir does require a specialized skill set, and choir members are generally expected to have musicianship and singing technique that exceeds that of the average parishioner. Fortunately, these are skills that can usually be built and nurtured through weekly rehearsals and quality instruction. The ability to read music quickly and easily, for example, is an essential skill for all choristers. With services occurring on a weekly basis, choirs are required to prepare a large repertoire in a short amount of time. Singers who struggle with reading music are likely to become overwhelmed. There are, however, many resources available to improve one's musicianship, from textbooks or workshops to voice or piano lessons. The more choral experience one has, the more focused these skills become. The motivated chorister is likely to improve significantly in a short amount of time.

QUESTIONS FOR REFLECTION AND DISCUSSION

1. When you next attend the Eucharist, pay particular attention to the anthem. Read it alongside the Gospel. How do the two texts complement one another? (Bonus: Find your choirmaster after the service. Ask him or her why that anthem was chosen.)

2. Think about the service you attend most often at your church. What does the choir mean to your experience of the liturgy?

3. Does your choir ever perform music that falls outside of the Anglican tradition? If so, what styles do they explore? Do you enjoy hearing these pieces? Why or why not?

Singing the Psalter

Rejoice in the LORD, you righteous; *
   it is good for the just to sing praises.
Praise the LORD with the harp; *
   play to him upon the psaltery and lyre.
Sing for him a new song; *
   sound a fanfare with all your skill
   upon the trumpet.
For the word of the LORD is right, *
   and all his works are sure.
He loves righteousness and justice; *
   the loving-kindness of the LORD
   fills the whole earth.

Psalm 33:1–5 (BCP 626)

The Psalter is a poetic translation of the book of Psalms intended for use in liturgical worship. Found in various translations in the many revisions of the Book of Common Prayer now used throughout the Anglican Communion, it is one of Anglicanism's greatest contributions to Christian literature. In addition to the text itself, the rich English tradition of singing the psalms in Anglican chant represents one of the Episcopal Church's most beloved traditions.

The psalms are meant to be *sung.* The Greek word ψαλμοί or *psalmoi* literally means "songs accompanied by string instruments." In addition, the rubrics preceding Psalms 75 and 76 are addressed to the choirmaster (or music leader), instructing him which song to use or that the psalm should be accompanied by strings. Singing the psalms is a feature of most Episcopal liturgies, from the smallest parish to the largest cathedral. While psalm singing is a part of the Eucharist, the tradition is particularly rich during daily Morning and Evening Prayer.

THE PSALMS

The Book of Psalms is part of both the Hebrew *Tanakh* and the Christian Old Testament. According to the *New Harvard Dictionary of Music,* "no other book of the Bible is so musically conceived or has left such a strong imprint on the music associated with prayer, praise, and thanksgiving."[15] It is widely regarded as the most treasured book in the scriptures, regularly read by Christians, Jews, and even the non-religious.

Although the psalms were historically attributed to King David, we do not know who wrote most of them. Composed over a vast period of time, the psalms express the feelings of the Hebrew people at various times in their tumultuous history. Many psalms date back to the early years of Israel and were probably sung at the First Temple of Jerusalem. Some may have been written as early as 900 BCE, and others describe particular events as disparate as the Babylonian Captivity (498–438 BCE) and the Maccabean Revolt (167–160 BCE). Eventually compiled into their present (and usual) 150 psalm collection, they have been regularly used in worship for well over two thousand years.

It is likely that Jesus and his disciples regularly prayed the psalms in their daily worship. Jesus directly echoes Psalms 22 and 31 in his words from the cross: "My God, my God, why have you forsaken me?" (Matthew 27:46 and Mark 15:34) and "Father, into your hands I commend my spirit" (Luke 23:46). The Passion narratives contain many references to the psalms.

The psalms are eclectic and cannot be neatly summarized. They touch on many themes, including God's care for the oppressed (Psalm 146), the experience of sorrow and grief (Psalm 42), pleas for help in times of trouble (Psalm 77), and of course praise and thanksgiving to God (Psalm 148). Psalm 119, by far the longest, is an alphabetical acrostic—a poem in which the first letter of each line spells out a word or message—written in praise of the law. Nor is God represented consistently throughout the psalms, which sometimes portray the Lord as a God of wrath and destruction and other times the source of great love and mercy. Many psalms were revised over the course of their collection and preservation, contributing to the complexity of the book.

In the Book of Common Prayer, there may be divisions noted within a psalm, signifying breaks in the poetry. These sections are grouped by theme. Psalm 68, for example, divides into three distinct parts: verses 1–20, 21–23, and 24–36. Original Latin titles also appear in the Book of Common Prayer, indicating again the historic, significant role the psalms have played in the daily prayer of the church.

In his "Preface to the Psalms," the great theologian and Reformation leader Martin Luther wrote, "The Psalter ought to be a precious and beloved book, if for no other reason than this: it promises Christ's death and resurrection so clearly—and pictures his kingdom and the condition and nature of all Christendom—that it might well be called a little Bible." A more thorough introduction to this "little Bible" may be found in *Conversations with Scriptures: The Psalms* (2013) by L. William Countryman or *Meditations on the Psalms for Every Day of the Year* (2003) by Barbara Cawthorne Crafton.

THE PSALTER: A BRIEF HISTORY

Miles Coverdale, in the Great Bible of 1539, produced a full English version of the book of Psalms that was published along with the 1549 Book of Common Prayer. Coverdale translated from Latin (rather than the original Hebrew), using a text that was based on the Septuagint, a translation of the Hebrew scriptures into Greek. The Psalter was directly incorporated into the Book of Common Prayer in subsequent revisions. In 1611, the Authorized King James Version of the Bible introduced another English translation of the Psalms, but the Coverdale translation was retained in the Church of England's 1662 prayer book.

The Psalter, as it appears in the Book of Common Prayer, is especially designed for singing. Verses are split in two—marked by an asterisk—reflecting the two-part versification form of the original Hebrew. The two halves of the psalm verse can relate to each other in various ways. The three most common relationships are often described as synonymous (similar), antithetic (contrasting), and synthetic (the second half is a logical expansion of the first), as explained in the instructions "Concerning the Psalter" in the 1979 Book of Common Prayer:

> The version of the Psalms that follows is set out in lines of poetry. The lines correspond to Hebrew versification, which is not based on meter or rhyme, but on parallelism of clauses, a symmetry of form and sense. The parallelism can take the form of similarity (The waters have lifted up, O Lord / the waters have lifted up their voice; / the waters have lifted up their pounding waves. *Psalm 93:4*), or of contrast (The Lord knows the ways of the righteous; / but the way of the wicked is doomed. *Psalm 1:6*), or of logical expansion (Our eyes look to the Lord our God, / until he show us his mercy. *Psalm 123:3*). (BCP 583)

The instructions go on to note that "the most common verse is a couplet, but triplets are very frequent, and quatrains are not unknown," though they are often divided into two verses. Each verse is divided into two parts, with an asterisk at the end of the first part so a distinct pause can be made while reading or chanting, thus priming the psalms to be sung in liturgical worship.

THE ROLE OF THE PSALMS IN WORSHIP

Psalms are prescribed by the Book of Common Prayer for use during all of the daily office and most liturgical services. The most profound liturgical use of the psalms, however, occurs during Morning and Evening Prayer. Over the course of a thirty-day cycle, the entire Psalter is sung in the daily office. Christopher Hill writes about the importance of singing the psalms daily:

> In the Anglican choral offices of Matins [Morning Prayer] and Evensong, the singing of the allocated portions of the Psalter on a daily basis to Anglican chant provides for many people the spiritual backbone of this continuum of worship. The Book of Psalms encompasses the whole gamut of human emotion: not only joy, praise, love, hope, and faith; but also sorrow, despair, fear, penitence, aggression, and revenge. When heard at its finest, sung in the ambience of a great cathedral or college chapel, and combined with the visual bonus of magnificent architecture, Anglican chant can assume a significance and inspiration that readily identifies it as an essential ingredient of worship, in addition to being an art-form in itself.[16]

Singing or listening to the psalms over a thirty-day cycle can be a deeply moving spiritual experience. There are fine recordings available and a variety of psalm tones, from simple to complex, for singing.

In the Book of Common Prayer, the psalms are organized into a thirty-day (monthly) cycle, with groups of psalms designated for morning and evening of each day. The psalms to be read on the morning of the first day of the month, for example, are Psalms 1–5 (BCP 585–589); the psalms for the evening of the first day are 6–8 (BCP 589–592). The Psalter is also divided into five "books," consistent with the 1611 King James Version of the Bible, where a doxology follows Psalms 41, 72, 89, and 106. The Book of Common Prayer retains this five-book division (see pages 585, 643, 687, 717, and 746. Note that the thirty-day rotation, however, functions independently and pays no attention to the Jacobean five-book structure: the boundary between the first two books in the biblical model, for instance, is between Psalms 41 and 42, which is right in the middle of Evening Prayer on Day 8 (BCP 643). For those who wish to read the Psalms at a more leisurely pace, an alternate seven-week cycle may be found in the daily office lectionary of the Book of Common Prayer (pages 933–1001).

On some occasions, selected canticles from the Book of Common Prayer may be substituted for the psalm. This occurs most often at eucharistic services during certain seasons of the church year (such as on the Third Sunday of Advent when the *Magnificat,* or Song of Mary, replaces the psalm).

SINGING THE PSALMS
Types of Psalm Recitation
The Book of Common Prayer, in its section entitled "Concerning the Psalter," outlines four specific ways in which the psalms can be recited (BCP 582).

1. *Direct recitation* refers to chanting an entire psalm in unison. This method is perhaps the most common, usually heard during the eucharistic liturgy.

2. *Antiphonal recitation* occurs when there is verse-by-verse alteration between groups of singers, such as between two sides of the choir or the choir and the congregation. Antiphonal recitations usually conclude with an antiphon (refrain) or—in the case of Morning or Evening Prayer—the Lesser Doxology (also known as the *Gloria Patri*).

3. *Responsorial recitation* refers to psalmody with verses sung by a cantor and refrains sung by the

choir and congregation. The *Venite* at Morning Prayer was historically sung responsorially.

4. *Responsive recitation* occurs when the reader alternates with the congregation in speaking the psalm.

The Book of Common Prayer encourages congregations to rotate recitation methods to avoid monotony, not using any one of these four recitations exclusively.

Plainchant

Plainchant refers to the non-metric (or rhythmically free) style of singing that dates back to the medieval era. Plainchant, as its name perhaps implies, features a single melody line. Gregorian chant is a well-known example of plainchant. S11 and S41 in *The Hymnal 1982* are plainchant versions of Psalm 100 (the Jubilate), but any psalm can be sung in plainchant. Bulletins will often have the texts of the psalms "pointed" (or notated) so that it is clear when to move to the next note. Pointing can be done in a variety of ways, such as through the use of boldface or horizontal slash marks within the text.

Anglican Chant

Anglican chant is a harmonized, four-part sung recitation of the text that utilizes set formulas for singing psalms (and sometimes canticles). Anglican chant formulas usually consist of a series of chords that can be used interchangeably with various psalm texts. The psalms are then pointed by the choirmaster or organist in order to reconcile speech patterns and significant words to the chant tone selected. More so than any other form of chant, the genre utilizes "speech rhythm," where delivery of the text imitates the natural flow of the English language. Rhythm is determined by the natural declamation of the text, as opposed to a strict "pulse" or meter. Well-sung Anglican chant will bring clarity and primacy to the text.

Anglican chant probably originated as harmonized Gregorian plainchant, but after the Reformation it evolved into its own distinct genre. The melody was moved to the top voice (rather than the tenor) and the harmonies followed tonal choral progressions. A standard "double chant" format also emerged: this two-part form of ten chords each could be further divided into two subphrases (4 + 6 chords in each half). Each half of each phrase opens with a "reciting chord," which is unmeasured and rhythmically free, after which the syllables progress toward a cadence. Each two-part phrase mimics the two-part poetic structure of the psalm verse (as published in the prayer book).

While this is complicated to explain in words, it is much easier to see and hear. The example on the opposite page is a standard notation of a psalm pointed in Anglican chant, in this case Psalm 15.[17] This example provides two possible formulas for singing the seven-verse psalm. The first (at the top) is a "single chant" (one phrase); the second is a standard "double chant." The single chant is sung to one verse of text, whereas the double chant requires two verses to complete. The formula—whichever is used—is then repeated until the psalm is completed. Vertical markings delineate measures, and brackets indicate the singing of multiple syllables on the same note. Asterisks correspond to the double bar lines in the middle of a phrase. The cross marking before the final verse indicates that the second half of the formula should be used to sing this verse (when using the standard double chant—it is a non-issue in single chant); this is common practice for a psalm with an odd number of verses.

In the supplemental service music section of *The Hymnal 1982,* several "simplified" Anglican chant formulas are provided (S409–S414). Simplified Anglican chant reduces a standard double formula to eight chords, as opposed to the usual twenty. These pared-down formulas are designed to encourage congregational participation, whereas the more complex standard formulas are often—but not always—sung by the choir

Psalm 15   *Domine, quis habitabit?*

29   *James Nares*

30   *David Hurd*

1 LORD, who may ' dwell in your ' tabernacle? *
  who may abide up'on your ' holy ' hill?

2 Whoever leads a blameless life and ' does what is ' right, *
  who ' speaks the ' truth from his ' heart.

3 There is no guile upon his tongue;
  he does no ' evil to his ' friend; *
  he does not heap con'tempt up'on his ' neighbor.

4 In his sight the ' wicked is re'jected, *
  but he honors ' those who ' fear the ' LORD.

5 He has sworn to ' do no ' wrong *
  and ' does not take ' back his ' word.

6 He does not give his money in ' hope of ' gain, *
  nor does he take a ' bribe a'gainst the ' innocent.

†7 Whoever ' does these ' things *
   shall ' never be ' over'thrown.

alone. If a church or cathedral invites its entire congregation
to participate in a full Anglican chant, then the music must
be printed in the bulletin with very clear pointing. Congregational singing of the psalm will probably also require the repetition of a formula throughout a liturgical season rather than
changing the formula from week to week (which many choirs
do).

Most Anglican chant formulas are double chants, reflecting
the original form of the Hebrew poetry. Triple chants (three
phrases) can exist, however, as can four-phrase quadruple
chants, though this latter form is quite rare. Most psalms do

not lend themselves well to double- and triple-formulas, but there are a few notable exceptions: Psalm 2, which is organized in a series of three-verse thematic units, works beautifully when sung to a triple chant, and Psalm 78 lends itself well to a quadruple chant.

Anglican chant is usually accompanied by the organ. It is the instrumentalist's responsibility to create an interesting palette of colors to support the singing, as well as highlighting specific words of the text with appropriate organ settings (a technique often called "text painting"). Confident choirs or congregations may sing some verses of the psalm *a cappella.*

Gelineau Chant
Gelineau chant, a congregational method of singing the psalms, was developed by the twentieth-century French Jesuit priest Joseph Gelineau. In Gelineau chant, a congregation sings an antiphon (refrain) between psalm verses, which are sung by a choir or cantor. Gelineau chants are also in a regular meter, unlike Anglican chant and plainchant. Although his psalm texts were originally taken from the French Jerusalem Bible, they can be adapted into a number of languages, including English. The antiphons are often paraphrases of hymn tunes.

Metrical Psalms
Metrical psalms are texts set to simple, hymn-like melodies. They are easy to sing, and encourage congregational partici-pation, finding great popularity among small parish churches as early as the sixteenth century. Metrical psalms originated with the Reformed movement during the sixteenth century, when John Calvin advocated for singable translations of songs in the vernacular. The first significant collection of metrical psalms was the 1562 *Geneva Psalter,* a French translation of the Psalter paired with 125 different melodies and intended for congregational singing. The popularity of metrical psalms soon spread. This inspired a number of early metrical Psalters

in English, beginning with *The Whole Book of Psalmes* (1562) by Thomas Sternhold and John Hopkins. Two other significant English compilations included Thomas East's *The Whole Booke of Psalmes* (1592) and Thomas Ravenscroft's 1621 collection of the same name. Nahum Tate and Nicholas Brady issued a widely used metrical Psalter—known as the *New Version*—in 1696.

The Bay Psalm Book (1640) was the first metrical Psalter published in the colonies, though as a nonconformist production it was never authorized for use in Anglican worship, which continued to use Sternhold and Hopkins, adding Tate and Brady after 1696. The first edition contained no music, but referred the singer to forty-eight tunes that were to be sung in combination with six metrical patterns. Music did not appear until the ninth edition of *The Bay Psalm Book* in 1698. Isaac Watts also published a rhymed collection entitled *The Psalms of David Imitated in the Language of the New Testament* (1719).

Congregational Participation

While the psalms may be sung by the choir alone, there are also many ways in which the congregation can be invited to participate. Four collections in particular should be mentioned. Alec Wyton's *The Anglican Chant Psalter* (1987) designates Anglican chant formulas for each psalm that are more suitable for congregational use. Bruce Ford's *Gradual Psalms* (2007) offer fully notated plainchant versions of the Psalter. *The Hymn Tune Psalter* (2008) by Carl P. Daw, Jr., and Kevin R. Hackett uses well-known hymn tunes as congregational antiphons. Finally, Keith Shafer's *Psalms Made Singable* (2009) notates full Anglican chant formulas, lining up the text with the repeated music, thus giving congregations easier access to the rich tradition of Anglican chant. Across the country, creative music ministers are continuing to find new ways of directly involving parishioners with liturgical psalm singing.

Q QUESTIONS FOR REFLECTION
AND DISCUSSION

1. Compare the Psalter of the 1979 Book of Common Prayer with the 1539 Coverdale translation (found in the 1928 version of the Book of Common Prayer, as well as other sources) and with newer translations your parish may use, such as *The Saint Helena Psalter* (2000). Which do you prefer, and why?

2. Read the complete Psalter as suggested by the Book of Common Prayer: twice a day (morning and evening) over a thirty-day period. Reflect on the experience. How has this daily devotional use of the psalms affected you spiritually?

3. The next time you attend a service at your parish, analyze how the psalm is sung. Is it sung in plainchant, to an Anglican chant formula, or some other way? Is the congregation invited to participate?

Morning and Evening Prayer (Matins and Evensong)

Be joyful in the LORD, all you lands; *
   serve the LORD with gladness
   and come before his presence with a song.
Know this: The LORD himself is God; *
   he himself has made us, and we are his;
   we are his people and the sheep of his pasture.
Enter his gates with thanksgiving;
   go into his courts with praise; *
   give thanks to him and call upon his Name.
For the LORD is good; his mercy is everlasting; *
   and his faithfulness endures from age to age.
Jubilate, Psalm 100 (BCP 729)

With the exception of the Holy Eucharist, Morning and Evening Prayer are the most common services offered by the Episcopal Church. Many churches observe these liturgies regularly; they may occur on a weekly basis, and some larger parishes even offer a daily Morning or Evening Prayer. The musical tradition behind each service—particularly Evening Prayer—is rich, which make these services a popular destination for parishioners (and non-Episcopalians) who value music as an important part of their worship.

THE MATINS AND EVENSONG TRADITION

The tradition of Morning Prayer (also called Matins) and Evening Prayer (also called Evensong) has its root in the eight canonical offices sung in the medieval monasteries of the Catholic Church. The eight original hours are:

1. Matins: sometime after midnight
2. Lauds: at daybreak
3. Prime: first hour (6 am)
4. Terce: third hour (9 am)
5. Sext: sixth hour (noon)
6. None: ninth hour (3 pm)
7. Vespers (early evening)
8. Compline (before retiring)

When the Book of Common Prayer replaced the Catholic liturgy during the English Reformation, Morning and Evening Prayer officially replaced the eight offices of the monastic tradition. This two-office tradition has endured throughout the church's long history. Morning Prayer was essentially a blend of Matins, Lauds, and Prime; Evening Prayer was a translation of Vespers, with a bit of Compline. In addition to these two principal prayer offices, the 1979 Book of Common Prayer includes the offices of noonday prayer (Sext) and Compline. While these latter two liturgies recommend certain psalms, they do not prescribe canticles in the same manner as the Morning and Evening Prayer liturgies.

Canticles are an essential ingredient of both Morning and Evening Prayer. Canticles—listed in the 1979 Book of Common Prayer on pages 47–53 and 85–96—are biblical and non-biblical texts that function like psalms as songs of praise or supplication. During the Reformation, it was typical to draw from a wide variety of canticles. After the 1662 revision of the prayer book, however, the use of canticles began to fall into a regular pattern known as the "short service." Over the period from 1660–1830, a familiar two-canticle arrangement for each prayer service solidified: Morning Prayer generally offered the *Te Deum laudamus* and the *Benedictus Dominus Deus* with a seasonal substitution of *Benedicite, omnia opera Domini* for the *Te Deum laudamus* during Lent. (The *Benedicite* became significantly less important after the 1979 prayer book revision.) Evening Prayer almost always included the *Magnificat* and the *Nunc dimittis,* an arrangement that remains in place today. These last two canticles especially were a source of great inspiration to Anglican composers, with hundreds of Evensong short services proliferating over the course of the nineteenth century and beyond.

THE MUSICAL STRUCTURE OF MORNING AND EVENING PRAYER

While some of the musical elements of Morning and Evening Prayer are the same as the Eucharist—anthems and psalms (usually sung to Anglican chant)—there are some unique musical components as well. We will begin with the non-canticle musical elements of Matins and Evensong. The Book of Common Prayer offers both of these liturgies in Rite I (BCP 37 and 61) and Rite II (BCP 75 and 115) formats.

Opening Preces and Response

The Opening *Preces* and Response (also called The Invitatory) is typically the first music sung during Morning and Evening Prayer, and the text varies slightly depending on the service. Morning Prayer consists of the following text, sung by the officiant and the people in responsorial plainchant:

> *Officiant*   Lord, open our lips.
> *People*   And our mouth shall proclaim your praise.

This variation is spoken at the beginning of Evensong:

Officiant   O God, make speed to save us.
People   O Lord, make haste to help us.

These words are followed immediately by the Lesser Doxology.

Lesser Doxology (Gloria Patri)
Immediately after the Opening *Preces* and Response, the people sing the Lesser Doxology. Also known as the *Gloria Patri,* the Lesser Doxology is distinct from the Great Doxology (*Gloria in excelsis,* found in the 1979 Book of Common Prayer as Canticles 6 and 20). There are many musical settings of the Lesser Doxology. The text is as follows:

> Glory to the Father, and to the Son, and to the
>   Holy Spirit:*
> as it was in the beginning, is now, and will be for ever.
>   Amen.

The *Gloria Patri* also follows the psalms and certain canticles of Morning and Evening Prayer. In the 1979 Book of Common Prayer, there is no distinction between the Rite I and Rite II versions of the Lesser Doxology.

Venite and Phos hilaron
An opening hymn of praise then follows the Lesser Doxology. In Morning Prayer, this will most often be the *Venite,* a modified version of Psalm 95 (BCP 44–45 and 82). *The Hymnal 1982* includes eleven settings of the *Venite* (S4–S7 and S34–S40). While the *Venite* has historically been a standard ingredient of Morning Prayer, the 1979 Book of Common Prayer allows for the substitution of Psalm 95 (BCP 724), the *Jubilate* (Psalm 100, BCP 45 and 82–83), or, during the Easter season, the *Pascha nostrum* (BCP 46 and 83).

During Evening Prayer, the *Phos hilaron* ("O Gracious Light") immediately follows the Lesser Doxology (BCP 64 and 118). In addition to the four settings in *The Hymnal 1982*

(S27 and S59–S61), there are many settings of this early non-biblical hymn text by both major and minor composers, usually intended to be sung by the choir alone.

Psalms and Canticles

Now the appointed psalms are sung, the first and second lessons (Old and New Testament readings) are read, and two canticles are sung. The canticles—which are idiomatic and distinct for Matins and Evensong—will be discussed in greater detail below.

The Apostles' Creed and the Lord's Prayer

Both Morning and Evening Prayer use the Apostles' Creed (BCP 53–54 and 96, 66 and 120). The creed is usually read but can be sung on a monotone pitch. The Lord's Prayer—also sometimes sung in monotone—immediately follows the Apostles' Creed.

Versicles and Responses

Also called the "Lesser Litany" or the "Suffrages," the Versicles and Responses that follow the Lord's Prayer are often sung, with settings available in *The Hymnal 1982* and elsewhere. In both Rite I and Rite II, there are two versions of the Versicles and Responses, labeled as Suffrages A (BCP 55 and 97–98, 67–68 and 121–122) and Suffrages B (BCP 55 and 98, 68 and 122). Suffrages A are the same at both Matins and Evensong, whereas the Suffrages B are unique to each office. After the praying of various collects, the liturgies conclude with a final Versicle and congregational Response.

THE MORNING PRAYER CANTICLES

Throughout most of the history of the Church of England and its sister churches, there have been three major canticles of Morning Prayer. The *Te Deum laudamus* was sung daily except in Lent, when it was replaced by the *Benedicite, omnia opera Domini* (A Song of Creation). *Benedictus Dominus Deus*

(The Song of Zechariah), the second canticle, could be replaced by the *Jubilate* (Psalm 100). The 1979 Book of Common Prayer allows for greater flexibility. In the current model, the *Jubilate* may substitute for the invitatory psalm (the *Venite*), and the *Te Deum laudamus* and *Benedictus Dominus Deus* comprise the standard two-canticle structure of Matins. Substitution canticles generally occur after the Old Testament reading during Advent, Lent, and Easter, with the standard substitution canticles being *Surge, illuminare* (BCP 87–88) in Advent, *Kyrie Pantokrator* (BCP 90–91) in Lent, and *Cantemus Domino* (BCP 85) in Easter. The table of suggested canticles for Morning Prayer can be found on page 144 of the Book of Common Prayer.[18]

Te Deum laudamus
Like the *Phos hilaron* and *Gloria in excelsis,* the *Te Deum laudamus* (BCP 52–53 and 95–96) is an early Christian hymn of praise. Originally ascribed to St. Ambrose and St. Augustine in the fourth century, the *Te Deum laudamus* is one of the most important canticles of Morning Prayer, often sung on Sundays and feast days after the New Testament reading except during Lent. On occasion, Anglican composers have paired this text with the *Jubilate* (Psalm 100) in Morning Prayer short service settings. As with most of the canticles, a large body of choral repertoire was written before 1979, so the Rite I version of the *Te Deum laudamus* is commonly heard in choral settings.

Benedictus Dominus Deus (The Song of Zechariah)
The *Benedictus Dominus Deus* is one of the three Gospel canticles, all of which appear in Luke. This text is sung by Elizabeth's husband Zechariah when his son is born (Luke 1:68–79), and appears in the Book of Common Prayer in both Rite I and Rite II versions (BCP 50–51 and 92–93). *Benedictus Dominus Deus* is sung on Sundays and feast days during Morning Prayer after the Old Testament reading except during

Advent and Lent, when it replaces the *Te Deum laudamus* after the New Testament reading.

Morning Prayer Short Service Settings

Although there are significantly more settings of the canticles of the Evening Prayer short service, the common Morning Prayer short service—the *Te Deum* and *Jubilate*—became a favorite for many composers, with famous settings by Henry Purcell, George Frideric Handel, Samuel Sebastian Wesley, Charles Villiers Stanford, and Herbert Howells, among others.

Alternate Morning Prayer Canticles

In addition to the two principal canticles of Matins—the *Te Deum laudamus* and the *Benedictus Dominus Deus*—there are options for other canticles during Morning Prayer as well. The Old Testament reading may be followed by one of the Old Testament canticles (8–11) or one of the Apocryphal canticles (1–2 and 12–14). After the New Testament reading, the *Gloria in excelsis* (6 and 20) or one of the Revelation canticles (18–19) may be sung. These alternatives may be found on page 144 of the Book of Common Prayer.

THE EVENING PRAYER CANTICLES

The *Magnificat* and *Nunc dimittis* are the standard canticles of Evening Prayer. Hundreds of major and minor composers have set these two canticles in musical pairings, and this body of evening services is perhaps the richest choral repertoire to emerge during the golden era of Anglican Church music, the period stretching from approximately 1830 to 1922.

Magnificat (The Song of Mary)

The *Magnificat*—along with the *Benedictus Dominus Deus* and the *Nunc dimittis*—is one of the three Gospel canticles. Also called The Song of Mary, it appears in the first chapter of the Gospel of Luke (1:46–55). Mary speaks these words to her cousin Elizabeth, who is pregnant with John the Baptist. Elizabeth praises Mary for her faith, and Mary responds with the *Magnificat*. It appears in the Book of Common Prayer in both Rite I and Rite II versions (BCP 65 and 119).

Nunc dimittis (The Song of Simeon)
The *Nunc dimittis*—the last of the three Gospel canticles (Luke 2:29–32)—appears in the Book of Common Prayer in both Rite I and Rite II versions (BCP 66 and 120). Also called The Song of Simeon, it is uttered by a devout Jew who had been promised by God that he would not die until he had seen the Savior. When Mary and Joseph visit the temple for the consecration of Jesus, Simeon holds the baby in his arms and praises God that at long last he had seen that promised Savior, who would be "a Light to enlighten the nations, and the glory of your people Israel."

Evening Prayer Short Service Settings
The evening service (pairings of the *Magnificat* with the *Nunc dimittis*) was one of the most important choral genres to emerge from the creative burst of Anglican church music during the nineteenth and early twentieth centuries. Settings are manifold, and evening services were composed by most of the greatest composers of English church music.

Alternate Evening Prayer Canticles
In addition to the two principal canticles of Evensong—the *Magnificat* and the *Nunc dimittis*—there are options for other canticles during Evening Prayer as well. Like Morning Prayer, the Old Testament reading may be followed by one of the Old Testament canticles (8–11) or one of the Apocryphal canticles (1–2 and 12–14). The New Testament reading, however, is always followed by either the *Magnificat* or the *Nunc dimittis*. These alternate canticle options for Evening Prayer can be found on page 145 of the Book of Common Prayer.

Q QUESTIONS FOR REFLECTION
  AND DISCUSSION

1. The Morning and Evening Prayer liturgies are similar in some ways, but very different in others. Which one usually speaks more strongly to you? Are you a "morning person" or an "evening person" when it comes to prayer?

2. The *Te Deum laudamus* and *Benedictus Dominus Deus* (The Song of Zechariah) are exclusively canticles of Morning Prayer, whereas the *Magnificat* (The Song of Mary) and *Nunc dimittis* (The Song of Simeon) only occur at Evening Prayer. Read through these four texts in the Book of Common Prayer. What do you see within the texts that makes them particularly appropriate for their location in the morning or evening?

3. Obtain a recorded Evensong service and listen to it in its entirety while following along with the Book of Common Prayer. (Notice the slight differences if you are listening to an English choir.) Which portions are sung? What musical textures and genres are you hearing? (For example: plainchant, Anglican chant, congregational singing, anthems, hymns, and so on)

The Festival of Nine Lessons and Carols: An Anglican Tradition

If ye would hear the angels sing
"Peace on earth and mercy mild,"
Think of him who was once a child,
On Christmas Day in the morning.

If ye would hear the angels sing,
Rise, and spread your Christmas fare;
'Tis merrier still the more that share,
On Christmas Day in the morning.

Christmas Carol by Dora Greenwell (1821–1882)

The annual Festival of Nine Lessons and Carols is one of the Episcopal Church's most beloved traditions. Originating in England, this unique service has also established itself in the United States, becoming a favorite perennial event in many parishes during the Advent and Christmas seasons. Lessons and Carols, however, is not a liturgical service, and is not found in the Book of Common Prayer, though *The Book of Occasional Services 2003* does include forms for a Festival of Lessons and Music for Advent and Christmas (BOS 31–34 and

38–41). How then, did this tradition develop, and why has it remained so popular?

LESSONS AND CAROLS: A BRIEF HISTORY

The Festival of Nine Lessons and Carols originated not as a festival at all, but as a simple service at Truro Cathedral in 1880. The legend is that Edward Benson, the Bishop of Truro (who would later become the Archbishop of Canterbury), organized a late evening service on Christmas Eve in an attempt to keep the men of Truro out of the pubs. After this initial service, the tradition seems to have gone dormant for many years. Thirty-eight years later, King's College, Cambridge held their first Festival of Nine Lessons and Carols on Christmas Eve in 1918.

While the reasons behind the development of the first Lessons and Carols services will never be definitively known, we can be certain that it was Benson who designed the original order of the service: nine short Bible readings interspersed with Christmas carols, choral offerings, and congregational hymns. According to Benson's son, the idea for nine lessons—the first of which would be read by a young chorister and the last by a bishop—originated with Somerset Walpole, later Bishop of Edinburgh. The readings heard during a Lessons and Carols service build from the Old Testament to the Gospels. Carols, hymns, and anthems are also carefully selected to complement the lessons. Using very different readings from the Easter Vigil, this pattern nonetheless makes similar connections between ancient scripture and the coming of Christ, which may have been Benson's deliberate intention.

THE KING'S COLLEGE TRADITION

The Lessons and Carols tradition as we experience it today owes virtually everything to King's College, Cambridge, where the service was revived on Christmas Eve in 1918, immediately after the conclusion of World War I and with the belief that a war-weary England was in desperate need of a more creative form of worship. The 1918 service established an annual tradition, and Lessons and Carols have been offered at King's College every year since, even during World War II.

The size of the choir at King's College has also remained remarkably consistent over the years. The original 1918 service utilized thirty singers, following the statutes laid down by King Henry VI in the fifteenth century. This roster included sixteen trebles and fourteen male choir members, all of whom were choral scholars and lay clerks. Beginning in 1927, the alto, tenor, and bass parts were assumed by undergraduates from King's College, and this remains true today. These select singers—who are called "choral scholars"—from the college also perform on their own in an ensemble as the Collegium Regale.

The Festival of Nine Lessons and Carols was immediately popular, and churches throughout England began appropriating the service. A radio broadcast of the service began in 1928, and this broadcast has become an annual tradition as well (with the single exception of 1930). The BBC began broadcasting the service overseas in the early 1930s, which helped to popularize the service in United States. American Public Media has broadcast the service nationally every year since 1979. Over the years, several television broadcasts have also been produced. Famous recordings on the Decca and EMI labels have also helped to establish the King's College Lessons and Carols tradition as a worldwide phenomenon that has spread far beyond the confines of the Anglican Church.

ABOUT THE NINE LESSONS

The Festival of Nine Lessons and Carols includes readings from the books of Genesis, Isaiah, Luke, Matthew, and John. Edward Benson selected the original nine lessons, and for the most part they are the lessons still in use today (with a minor revision to the order in 1919). At King's College, all readings are from the 1611 Authorized King James Version of the Bible. Read interspersed with one or two musical selections, the nine lessons (with the summary descriptions that appear in the annual Lessons and Carols booklet published by King's College) are:

First Lesson (Genesis 3:8–19): *God tells sinful Adam that he has lost the life of Paradise and that his seed will bruise the serpent's head.*

Second Lesson (Genesis 22:15–18): *God promises the faithful Abraham that in his seed shall all the nations of the earth be blessed.*

Third Lesson (Isaiah 9:2, 6–7): *The prophet foretells the coming of the Saviour.*

Fourth Lesson (Isaiah 11:1–3a, 4a, 6–9): *The peace that Christ will bring is foreshown.*

Fifth Lesson (Luke 1:26–35, 38): *The angel Gabriel salutes the Blessed Virgin Mary.*

Sixth Lesson (Luke 2:1, 3–7): *St Luke tells of the birth of Jesus.*

Seventh Lesson (Luke 2:8–16): *The shepherds go to the manger.*

Eighth Lesson (Matthew 2:1–12): *The wise men are led by the star to Jesus.*

Ninth Lesson (John 1:1–14): *St John unfolds the great mystery of the Incarnation.*

The hymns that begin and end the Festival at King's College also remain consistent from year to year. The processional hymn is always "Once in Royal David's City" (IRBY), the first stanza of which is sung *a cappella* by a young chorister; the second stanza is sung by the choir, and the organ and congregation join beginning with the third stanza. "O Come All Ye Faithful" (ADESTE FIDELES) is always sung after the ninth lesson, after which the Dean offers a final collect and blessing. "Hark the Herald Angels Sing" (MENDELSSOHN) concludes the service, triumphantly ushering in Christmas Day. To many, these three hymns are the very essence of the Lessons and Carols tradition.

Likewise, a tradition has developed around the assignment of readings. There is always a progression from a boy chorister to the Provost of the College—the youngest child to the most prominent and established adult. A representative from the City of Cambridge always reads the fourth lesson, and the director of music always reads the seventh lesson.

While many parishes adhere to the King's College model when offering their own Festival of Lessons and Carols, others freely adapt the service to suit their own needs. In the United States the New Revised Standard Version translation of the scripture readings usually replaces the King James Version, and alternate lessons also may be substituted.

What Is a Carol?

The answer to this question can be either complex or simple depending on whether one is a musicologist or a parishioner. The origins of the English carol date back to the medieval era as a popular tune sung by commoners with a quasi-religious text. The genre proliferated during the Renaissance era, and the archetypal carol was a lively Renaissance tune with a refrain, usually sung during Advent or Christmas (and sometimes Easter). Today, hymns and anthems with a specifically Christmas-themed text are usually labeled as carols, regardless of whether they have a refrain.

Advent Lessons and Carols

Many parishes choose to offer Lessons and Carols during Advent rather than on Christmas Eve. Reasons for this vary: it may be a matter of practicality, a desire to more fully observe Advent, or a preference for celebrating the Eucharist on Christmas Eve.

While there are many similarities between an Advent and Christmas Eve Lessons and Carols, there are of course many differences as well. Most noticeable is the selection of different hymns for the program. While "Once in Royal David's City" (IRBY) and "Hark! the Herald Angels Sing" (MENDELSSOHN) might be essential in the King's College tradition, they are not hymns that are liturgically appropriate during Advent, and thus are not used. The lessons also tend to be different; alternate ones from Jeremiah and the Apocryphal book of Baruch are common, but scripture choices are more likely to vary from parish to parish. Episcopal choirmasters tend to be eclectic in their choices when selecting carols and anthems, all the while observing the seasonal distinctions of Advent as a time of anticipation rather than of incarnation.

QUESTIONS FOR REFLECTION AND DISCUSSION

1. The nine scripture readings that are historically read during the Festival of Nine Lessons and Carols are a result of tradition and are not prescribed in any prayer book. As a result, alternate readings may be substituted freely. If you have attended a service of Lessons and Carols, which of the lessons do you remember most clearly? Why?

2. Recordings of the King's College Festival of Nine Lessons and Carols are ubiquitous. Aquire one and listen to it. Do you feel a connection to this thoroughly English experience, or is there something mysterious or foreign about it?

3. Read the nine lessons and carols in both the King James and New Revised Standard Version translations. What differences do you see? Which translation resonates more for you in this particular service?

Major Works: Oratorios, Passions, and Cantatas

Cross of Jesus, cross of sorrow,
where the blood of Christ was shed,
perfect Man on thee did suffer,
perfect God on thee has bled!

from The Crucifixion *by John Stainer;*
Hymn 160, Stanza 1, CROSS OF JESUS

Sacred choral repertoire occupies an important place in the history of music. While many of these works were intended for liturgical use, others were long narrative works on biblical themes intended for public concerts and known as oratorios. Two closely related genres—both of which had their roots in Lutheranism—are the Passion and the sacred cantata. Passions and cantatas are similar in some ways to the oratorio, but are often performed in churches, either taking the place of a liturgy or included in the liturgy. In addition, liturgical texts—such as Mass ordinary settings and Requiem Mass settings—have captured the fascination of many of the great choral composers in history; these major works are close cousins to the oratorio.

Although many of these works (with two important exceptions) are not necessarily a part of the Anglican choral tradition, Episcopal churches still program these pieces regularly. Often performed as concerts during appropriate times of the church year, these works may require guest instrumentalists and soloists, making them large and exciting events for parishes. In addition, many choirs regularly draw from these major works, incorporating excerpts into their repertoire as anthems and as liturgical material for soloists.

ORATORIOS, PASSIONS, CANTATAS, AND SACRED LATIN WORKS

Major works can exist in several different "flavors." Before proceeding further, it is worth spending a bit of time defining each of these subgenres of choral music. As all these genres and works are often collectively assumed under a broad definition of "oratorio," we will begin our discussion there.

Oratorios

An oratorio includes music for chorus, orchestra, and soloists. Oratorios generally have a biblical or religious narrative but are written for the concert hall rather than liturgical worship. Unlike opera, oratorios are generally not staged and do not feature sets and costumes. The oratorio proper is always set in the vernacular, although a loose and practical definition includes some Latin works as well.

The earliest oratorio experiments were Italian baroque works, but the genre became increasingly popular and soon spread to other countries, particularly Germany and England. The most important composer of oratorio during the baroque era (or perhaps any era) was the German-born English composer George Frideric Handel, who devoted himself almost exclusively to the genre during the later part of his long career in London. Altogether, Handel wrote a total of twenty-one oratorios. *Messiah*—by far his most famous—still receives thousands of performances annually during the month of De-

116   *Welcome to the Church Music and* The Hymnal 1982

cember. Churches large and small perform the Christmas portion (Part I) as the holiday approaches, many of them hosting "*Messiah* Sing-Alongs," which invite the community to join in on the choral portions.

During the classical era, Joseph Haydn composed the most important oratorios with *Die Schöpfung* (*The Creation,* 1798) and *Die Jahreszeiten* (*The Seasons,* 1801), and Felix Mendelssohn became the romantic era's most important oratorio composer with *Paulus,* Op. 36 (*St. Paul,* 1836) and *Elias,* Op. 70 (*Elijah,* 1846). In the twentieth century, England remained most devoted to the genre, with four essential oratorios: *The Dream of Gerontius,* Op. 38 (1900) by Edward Elgar, *Belshazzar's Feast* (1931) by William Walton, *A Child of Our Time* (1944) by Michael Tippett, and the *War Requiem* (1962) by Benjamin Britten.

Passions

A Passion is a specific type of oratorio that recounts the arrest, trial, and crucifixion of Jesus Christ. Because of the subject matter, Passions can be used in a liturgical context—usually as standalone "services" due to their length—and are most appropriately performed during Holy Week, ideally on Good Friday.

Passion settings have been a part of the Christian church for centuries. Some plainsong settings date back to the medieval era. While there are a number of Renaissance examples that predate them, the earliest Passions that remain a part of the repertoire are the Lutheran Passions of Heinrich Schütz; Schütz composed settings of the *St. John, St. Luke,* and *St. Matthew* Passions in 1665 and 1666. The two surviving Passions of Johann Sebastian Bach—the *St. John Passion,* BWV 245 (1724) and the *St. Matthew Passion,* BWV 244 (1727)— represent the apotheosis of the genre. Sung in German and clocking in at a running time of two and a half and three and a half hours, respectively, they are the province of only the most experienced choirs and generally require professional soloists and instrumentalists.

After the baroque era, the Passion fell out of favor as a genre of choice for many of the greatest composers. Several Anglican Passions, however, emerged in England beginning in the late nineteenth century; *The Crucifixion* (1887) by John Stainer and *Olivet to Calvary* (1904) by John Henry Maunder are the two works that have secured their place in the repertoire.

Cantatas

The term "cantata" has meant different things at different times in music history. In its earliest incarnation during the seventeenth and eighteenth centuries, a cantata was a multi-movement piece for voice and *continuo* (a very small instrumental ensemble usually consisting of a bass instrument—such as a viol or modern cello—and a keyboard instrument). These cantatas were usually settings of secular texts in Italian and French. The early solo cantatas of George Frideric Handel are of this type.

Cantatas entered the sacred choral repertoire as part of Lutheran church music in the eighteenth century. These cantatas were frequently based on chorale tunes (Lutheran hymn tunes), which provide some of the melodic material for the work. The full chorale is then presented as the last movement of the cantata. Soloists offer their own numbers between choral movements. The roughly two hundred sacred cantatas of Johann Sebastian Bach are quintessential examples of this genre.

In later eras, a cantata was simply a label used to describe a sacred work for soloists, chorus, and orchestra (or organ). These cantatas are still in several movements but are usually shorter than a full-length oratorio. There are numerous examples in the contemporary church music repertoire, including the *Christmas Cantata* (1957) of Daniel Pinkham. In contemporary practice, cantatas are usually performed as standalone concerts. Occasionally excerpts from cantatas are offered during liturgical services as well.

Sacred Latin Works

The Mass is also a musical genre, referring to a setting of the Mass ordinary (the five texts of the Eucharist that do not change according to the liturgical calendar). These are the *Kyrie, Gloria, Credo, Sanctus,* and *Agnus Dei.* A sixth part, the *Benedictus,* is actually part of the *Sanctus,* but is often set as a different movement or section of the Mass in musical settings. Other parts of the five sections may be broken off into separate movements; Bach's *B Minor Mass,* BWV 232 (1749), for example, utilizes twenty-seven separate movements to set the texts of the five portions of the ordinary.

There are many medieval and Renaissance Mass settings. These Masses were polyphonic and *a cappella* or unaccompanied. Instrumentally accompanied sacred vocal music did not take hold until the baroque era (beginning around the year 1600). Composers from the baroque era onward frequently set the ordinary as five-movement choral-orchestral works. The most famous Mass settings from this era include those by Joseph Haydn, Wolfgang Amadeus Mozart, Ludwig van Beethoven, and Franz Schubert.

The Requiem Mass includes additional texts beyond the Mass ordinary, specific to the burial office. The most famous settings of the Latin Requiem Mass include those by Mozart, Hector Berlioz, Giuseppe Verdi, Gabriel Fauré, and Maurice Duruflé. *Ein deutsches Requiem,* Op. 45 (1868) by Johannes Brahms is a unique twist on the Requiem genre. He entitled it "A German Requiem," preferring to set German biblical texts of his own choosing rather than the traditional Latin texts. In the twentieth century, Benjamin Britten, Paul Hindemith, and John Rutter similarly experimented with nontraditional Requiem texts.

Many other sacred Latin works of varying lengths have also found their way into the repertoire of church choirs. Some of the most popular are the *Stabat Mater* and the Latin versions of the *Te Deum* and *Magnificat* canticles, all of which have been set many times by both major and minor composers. Many shorter Latin works have enjoyed frequent settings by composers; the most popular include *Ave Verum Corpus* and the four Marian antiphons: *Alma Redemptoris Mater, Ave Regina Caelorum, Regina Coeli,* and *Salve Regina.*

ANGLICAN PASSIONS

During the latter half of the nineteenth century and the beginning of the twentieth, there was a thriving body of English language oratorios and cantatas by Anglican composers that were performed regularly by Episcopal church choirs. Unfortunately, most of these have fallen into complete obscurity, perhaps because of their (largely) derivative nature to the great European masterworks by major composers, which are judged by most historians to be superior in musical quality. Two notable exceptions, however, have persevered: *The Crucifixion* (1887) by John Stainer and *Olivet to Calvary* (1904) by John Henry Maunder.

Rightfully subcategorized as "Anglican Passions," these two oratorios offer a distinctly English twist on the Passion genre. Both composers imitate Bach in their use of chorale (hymn) tunes, a tenor soloist (as the evangelist/narrator), and a bass soloist (as the voice of Jesus). Unlike Bach, however, the works are scored for organ accompaniment and have choral parts that are capable of being performed by good amateur choirs. This accessibility has made them appealing works to smaller parishes and has helped to perpetuate their longevity. Throughout much of the twentieth century, Episcopal churches hosted annual performances of *The Crucifixion* and *Olivet to Calvary* on alternate years during Holy Week. Although this tradition has slowed down considerably, these are still two works worthy of discussion and performance by Episcopal church choirs.

Stainer's The Crucifixion (1887)

John Stainer was one of the most important figures in nineteenth-century Anglican church music. A prolific composer, he also served many years as organist at St. Paul's Cathedral in London, later becoming a professor of music at Oxford University. His success and fame throughout England brought him many honors, including being knighted by Queen Victoria in 1888.

Today, Stainer is primarily remembered as the composer of *The Crucifixion,* beloved in part due to its emphasis on congregational participation. In particular, Stainer modeled his work after Johann Sebastian Bach, who used congregational chorale tunes in his *St. Matthew Passion* and *St. John Passion.* Bach's inspiration is most keenly felt in Stainer's five hymns, which function in the same way that Bach's chorales do in his Passions. In addition to allowing for congregational participation, they also add gravity and poignancy to the drama, directly commenting and meditating upon the action. The five hymns include "Cross of Jesus" (No. 5), "Holy Jesu, by Thy Passion" (No. 10), "Jesus, the Crucified" (No. 13), "I Adore Thee" (No. 15), and "All for Jesus" (No. 20), all with original tunes by Stainer. "Cross of Jesus" is also included in *The Hymnal 1982* (CROSS OF JESUS, 160). In addition, choirs frequently present one of Stainer's choruses from this work, "God So Loved the World," as an anthem during the Lenten season or Holy Week. *The Crucifixion* has been recorded several times; notable recordings include those by the BBC Choir, St. Paul's Cathedral Choir, and the Choir of Claire College, Cambridge.

Maunder's Olivet to Calvary (1904)

Over the course of his career, John Henry Maunder was the organist and choirmaster at a number of churches in Forest Hill, Syndenham, Blackheath, and Sutton. Like Stainer, Maunder is primarily remembered today through his most famous work, *Olivet to Calvary,* which was composed in 1904.

Like *The Crucifixion,* there is an emphasis on congregational participation, with three hymns that are intended to be sung by the congregation: "Just As I Am" (in No. 4), "Thy Will Be Done" (in No. 6), and "Rock of Ages (in No. 10), all with original tunes by Maunder. *Olivet to Calvary* is divided in two large parts and ten "locations" that take the reader from the path to Jerusalem to Gethsemane to Calvary.

INTEGRATING ORATORIO EXCERPTS
AS ANTHEMS AND SOLOS
Incorporating major works into Episcopal liturgies can be challenging, as the Book of Common Prayer rubrics are not designed to accommodate large-scale works. Excerpts, however, can sometimes work, especially as anthems. The practice of incorporating choral anthems from oratorios into liturgical settings began during the Georgian era (1714–1830), when the sacred major works of Handel, Mozart, and Haydn were immensely popular throughout England. Handel's *Messiah,* for instance, organizes itself neatly into the seasons of Advent, Christmas, Lent, and Eastertide. The major oratorios of Felix Mendelssohn—*St. Paul* and *Elijah*—are also ripe with anthem fodder, and many Episcopal churches regularly use these choral excerpts as anthems. "How Lovely Is Thy Dwelling Place" by Johannes Brahms, which is the fourth and central movement of *Ein deutsches Requiem,* has also become a staple for Episcopal church choirs. (Note the similarity between this text and Vaughan Williams's "O How Amiable," discussed earlier.)

Solo excerpts from major works can also be incorporated. Regardless of their size, many Episcopal church choirs have a small group of professional section leaders and often considerable vocal talent among their volunteers. Sacred arias generally draw from the same oratorios listed above; the solo movements of Bach's sacred cantatas are one of the best ways to insert Bach's vocal music into the Sunday morning liturgy. Some solo offerings are not from larger works. Franz Schubert's "Ave Maria" (1825) and Alfred Hay Malotte's "The Lord's Prayer" (1935) and "The Beatitudes" (1938) are three often-performed solos that fall into this latter category. For a progressive American "twist," the twentieth-century composer Charles Ives has also set many hymn texts.

Q QUESTIONS FOR REFLECTION
  AND DISCUSSION

1. How many of the major works discussed in this chapter have you heard? Are there any composers mentioned here whose names you do not recognize? Try searching the internet for some of these names and famous works, and enjoy discovering some of the greatest choral music in the repertoire.

2. Stainer's *The Crucifixion* and Maunder's *Olivet to Calvary* are different works within the somewhat forgotten genre of the Anglican Passion. Obtain recordings of each and listen to both in their entirety. List some similarities between the two works, and list some differences. Think about both the text and the music. If you have a preference, which work do you prefer, and why?

3. Does worship in your parish ever incorporate vocal soloists? If so, how are they used? What kind of repertoire do they sing? When in the service are they used?

Organs and Organists

They take the timbrel and harp,
and rejoice at the sound of the organ.

Job 21:12 (KJV)

Since the earliest days, the pipe organ has played a central role in Anglican liturgy. Most of the choral and congregational repertoire—including anthems, psalms, and hymns—have historically been accompanied by the organ.

A good organ is designed and built for the space it inhabits. It is neither too small nor too big, and its sound perfectly fills the architecture of the space. Because the organ's primary role is to support congregational singing, the participation of the people in song is often linked to the quality of the instrument. Great organs attract great organists to play on them, and great organs encourage great music-making.

ORGAN BASICS: THE LEAST YOU NEED TO KNOW

The organ is not a standardized instrument. Organs come in various sizes; the simplest organ may have one keyboard, whereas the largest will have five or more. Built for specific rooms, every organ will have a unique design and layout. There are also national traditions: German, French, Dutch, English, Spanish, Italian, and American organs will all have their own specific features.[19] Here is an introduction to some of the basic components of pipe organs.

Action

The organ is a wind instrument, operated by pipes mounted on a "windchest." The "action" of an organ refers to how the valves in the windchest operate. There are three different types of action: "tracker" action describes a direct mechanical connection to the keys; "direct electronic" action describes the use of electromagnets wired to contacts under the keys; and "electro-pneumatic" action describes the use of small leather pouches, each of which collapses under the air pressure within the windchest. This last type of action also uses an electromagnet wired to contacts under the keys (hence the label electro-pneumatic). All pipe organs can be categorized according to these three types of action.

Wind Supply

Modern organs supply wind via an electric blower. Historically, delivering wind through an organ was a more complex endeavor. Nineteenth-century organs used bellows that were operated either through steam or waterpower. Prior to that, "organ pumpers" were often hired to manually pump the bellows of an organ.

Ranks

A rank is a series of similar pipes of varying length. Within a single rank, there is one pipe for each note of a keyboard. Therefore, if a manual, or keyboard, encompasses five octaves, those sixty-one notes will require sixty-one separate pipes. The longest pipe of a rank produces the lowest note, and the standard length is 8 feet (corresponding to the lowest C of an organ keyboard). Therefore, a 16-foot pipe will produce a note one octave lower and a 32-foot pipe will produce a note two octaves lower, while a 4-foot pipe will produce a note one octave higher and a 2-foot pipe will produce a note two octaves higher.

The smallest organs may only have one or two ranks of pipes, whereas the largest organs may have fifteen or more ranks. The bigger the space an organ inhabits, the more ranks are necessary to fill the space. A general rule of thumb is five ranks of pipes for every one hundred people. Therefore, a nave that seats three hundred will probably require an organ of fifteen ranks.

Stops

A stop usually controls a single rank of pipes. A stop is essentially a unique sound or "color"; no two stops sound alike. Stops have different timbres and tone qualities that correspond to specific pipes and registers. A stop usually has both a name and a length, such as Principal 8'.

Registration

Registration refers to the art of employing several stops simultaneously to achieve unique colors on the organ. An organist will often—if not always—employ multiple registration combinations within a single piece of music. Some composers are specific about organ registrations for a particular piece, whereas others are not. Even if a composer is specific, the organist may be playing on an instrument for which the piece was not originally written, requiring creativity and skill on the part of the organist to devise appropriate registration choices.

Mutations and Mixtures

In simple terminology, mutations refer to harmonies—usually at the intervals of thirds or fifths—that sound along with regular unison and octave intervals. A mixture is an organ stop with two or more pipes for each note, always sounding pitches at the octave or twelfth (octave and a fifth). The purpose of a mixture is to add brilliance, intensity, and clarity to the sound.

Flue Pipes
The flue pipe is the most common type of pipe found in an organ. In a flue pipe, the wind passes through a toe hole in the pipe, thus creating a vibrating column of air within the body of the pipe (similar to a recorder or whistle). They can create a wide variety of timbres depending on their voicing and scaling; tapered, open, stopped or half-stopped, and harmonic are just a few varieties. Flue pipes are often grouped into three categories according to their tone qualities: principals, strings, and flutes. The majority of an organ's stops will usually fall into one of these three major categories of flue pipes.

Reed Pipes
Reed pipes generate sound via a thin, metal tongue that acts as a reed vibrating against the open side of a metal or wood shallot (similar to a clarinet or saxophone mouthpiece). Tone quality is determined by the length (full or fractional), shape (conical or cylindrical), and diameter of the resonator. Reed stops that are used with one another and with principal flue pipes are called chorus reeds, and reed stops that can be used to play single-line melodies are called solo reeds.

Keyboards (Manuals and Pedalboard)
Organs usually have multiple keyboards; the larger the organ, the more keyboards the instrument will have. Keyboards controlled by the organist's hands are called manuals, whereas the large floor keyboard controlled by the feet is called the pedalboard. Most modern manuals encompass five octaves (sixty-one notes) and most pedalboards encompass two octaves and a fifth (thirty-twonotes). Some historical organs built in previous centuries have shorter manuals and pedalboards.

Divisions (Swell, Great, and Choir/Positive)
Each of the organ's keyboards controls a division, an independent part of the organ with its own windchest, key action,

and ranks of pipes. A division functions as its own organ. In American and English organs, the three divisions are generally labeled as swell, great, and choir (or positive).

The great is the main division of the organ, possessing the most dominant and frequently used principal stops. The choir is a diminution of the great division, containing flute and principal stops that are lighter in tone quality than the great. The swell division is named because the pipes are usually placed in an enclosure or "swell box" that can be opened or closed via a swell pedal; the swell is the division most likely to contain reed stops. In some organs, a pedal is a fourth division, but pedalboards on many smaller organs borrow significantly from the other three divisions.

Couplers

The various divisions of the organ can be connected to one another via coupling mechanisms. Couplers (as they are called) allow a designated manual to control a different set of ranks. For instance, a "swell to great" coupler allows the swell division to be played by the great manual. Couplers also allow the organist to combine stop combinations from various divisions, enhancing the potential for interesting registration choices.

Pistons (Combination and Reversible)

Most organs have combination pistons, which are a series of numbered buttons below the manuals. Pressing these buttons allows the organist to access a preselected (programmed) combination of stops, thus allowing for quick registration changes while playing. Toe pistons also allow the organist to rapidly change the pedal registration combinations as well. A reversible piston allows the organist to instantly access the full-organ combination; if pressed again, it returns to the previously selected registration.

Console
The console is the area where the organist sits, consisting of all manuals, the pedalboard, and stop/piston controls.

Casing
The casing refers to the outer shell of an organ, behind which exist the working mechanics of the organ itself (the pipes, action, and wind system). In addition to enhancing the look and aesthetic value of the organ, the casing also plays an important role acoustically, assisting the organ with its blend and projection into the room. The visual portion of the casing is called the façade, which will usually complement the architectural style of the building. Some of the pipes on the façade may be non-functional and solely for decorative purposes.

Builder
Organ building is a highly specialized art form, and the brand name of an organ carries considerable weight in the industry. In the United States, important centers of organ building were established in major Northeastern cities beginning in the nineteenth century. Important Boston organ builders included William Goodrich, Thomas Appleton, Ernest Skinner, and the Simmons, Stevens, and Hook brothers; New York builders included Thomas Hall, Henry Erben, and the Roosevelt brothers. J. T. Austin was an important Hartford builder, and Walter Holtkamp of Cleveland also built some important organs. American organs are based on a variety of European models, incorporating a wide range of styles and concepts.

ORGAN REPERTOIRE
The organ repertoire is vast, encompassing many countries and centuries. It is also profoundly interdenominational, and much of it was not written for liturgical use at all. Although Episcopal church choirs have historically recognized Anglican choral music as their core repertoire, Episcopal organists have generally drawn upon a wide variety of repertoire regardless

of the composer's nationality or the instruments for which the pieces were originally written. While there is a strong body of English organ literature, the most important composers of organ music were in fact German and French. Johann Sebastian Bach, for example, was Lutheran, but is perhaps the most frequently played composer by Episcopal organists.

Organ pieces may be given a wide variety of labels and subgenres, such as prelude, fantasia, toccata, and fugue (to name only a few). Articulating the differences between these various types of pieces becomes technical in nature and beyond the scope of this chapter. One of these subgenres, however—the voluntary—is worthy of mention. The voluntary is a distinctly English organ piece that is performed or improvised before worship. While there are many composed voluntaries in the organ repertoire, most have a spontaneous quality mimicking improvisation. The earliest examples of the genre date as early as the sixteenth century, and the composition of voluntaries persisted into the nineteenth. The most important composers of voluntaries in the seventeenth, eighteenth, and early nineteenth centuries include William Croft, Thomas Roseingrave, Maurice Greene, William Boyce, John Stanley, John Bennett, Samuel Wesley, and Thomas Adams. Although historically an English genre, voluntaries have been appropriated by a variety of other denominations while still being performed regularly at Episcopal churches.

ORGANISTS

As the organist has profound influence over worship, securing a quality organist is a significant responsibility. Most Episcopal churches that are large enough to employ a full-time musician hire a single person as an organist–choirmaster. Two half-time positions (for a separate organist and choirmaster) are also a possibility, and while this arrangement has its advantages— allowing both musicians to explore a particular area of expertise—a "split position" may also depend on the musicians finding other full- or part-time work within the community.

It is sometimes better for the church for the principal musician to be dedicated to his or her parish work full-time.

Most organists are also skilled piano players, as the piano is the standard instrument used in choral rehearsals (which generally take place in the choir room, not the chancel area or choir loft). In addition to playing the organ, intimate knowledge of organ literature, the choral repertoire, and vocal/choral technique are quintessential skills. Last—and perhaps most important—the organist has a pastoral role in the church as one of the leaders of worship. A great organist will not only have the musical skills to do his or her job well, but will also be viewed by the choir and parishioners as an excellent colleague and spiritual companion. The right organist for a particular parish is a treasure.

Organ Recitals

A quality organ is a significant investment. Churches that build new organs or restore old ones will usually sponsor a concert at the dedication of the instrument, inviting a world-class recitalist to perform. Organ dedications are major events and can be a landmark community-building experience in a church's life. In addition, many churches also sponsor organ concerts as part of a regular recital series. These recitals often function as ecumenical events, inviting community members to experience the music-making. Churches often expand their recital series to include a variety of other musical events, including various instrumentalists, vocalists, and guest ensembles. In recent years, musicians specializing in non-classical styles have begun to integrate themselves into these recitals as well.

Q QUESTIONS FOR REFLECTION AND DISCUSSION

1. The next time you attend worship, arrive early and examine the organ. Where is the console? Is the façade decorative, or are the pipes active? (If you do not know the answers, ask your organist! He or she will most likely be happy to talk with you about the instrument after the service.)

2. Listen intently to your organist playing the preludes and postludes to the service. Note the composers of each piece. How does the character of each selection relate to the season, or the "theme" of the lectionary's biblical readings for that particular day?

3. If your church has an organ recital series, make every effort to attend these concerts. Seek out other organ concerts in your area and beyond. Most major metropolitan areas offer ample opportunities to hear some of the best organists in the world at inexpensive ticket prices.

Other Episcopal Traditions

Sing to the LORD a new song; *
  sing to the LORD, all the whole earth.
Sing to the LORD and bless his Name; *
  proclaim the good news of his salvation
  from day to day.

Psalm 96:1–2 (BCP 725)

Episcopalians—perhaps more so than members of other denominations—cling steadfastly to tradition. Perhaps due to our common prayer and corporate worship tendencies, it is difficult to find a parish that does not make use of *The Hymnal 1982*. In fact, a survey published in 2012 affirms that 95.5 percent of churches surveyed still use the official hymnal at least once a week.[20] Musically, Episcopalians in general tend to be among the most formal and traditional of all Christian denominations.

Parishes *do* change and adapt, however. It is simply a matter of time, and as the Episcopal Church enters the twenty-first century, this reverence of tradition is changing. Many are exploring a range of musical styles within liturgical worship to great success.

The Episcopal Church prides itself on being welcoming and inclusive, and the explorations discussed here are just some of the many ways in which this spirit is playing out in musical circles within the church. Both ecumenical and broadly Anglican, the Episcopal Church is finding its worship incorporating tunes and musical styles from other denominations and traditions, as well as those from sister Anglican communities across the globe.

TAIZÉ

Taizé is an ecumenical monastic community located in the village of Taizé, Saône-et-Loire, Burgundy, France. It was founded in 1940 by the Swiss-born Brother Roger Schutz, who envisioned an inclusive community that emphasized prayer and meditation. Today, Taizé is comprised of more than one hundred men from many nations and denominations. Brother Roger was a prolific writer, and the philosophy of the Taizé community is well documented.

Although the term narrowly refers to the religious community itself, Taizé also defines a specific body of music composed by and for the Taizé community and the thousands who make a pilgrimage there each year. Based on chant, songs from Taizé feature simple repeated melodies, harmonies that can be easily improvised, and texts that lend themselves to use in liturgical worship. The founding composers of the Taizé repertoire included Jacques Berthier—a Parisian composer and organist at Église Saint-Ignace, the Jesuit church in Paris—and Joseph Gelineau. These two men are credited with conceiving and shaping the repertoire's style and liturgical use. Because the chants were designed to be used within an intentionally international community, a variety of languages are used (Latin, English, Spanish, French). Each text is short and repetitive, allowing their use without words or music in hand.

A Taizé service can be an intensely spiritual experience. The musical simplicity invites participation. Since no musical scores are needed, participants are free to close their eyes and become a part of the musical fabric. The repetition of the same chant for an extended period of time makes the experience of singing the music of Taizé introspective and meditative. Prayer and scripture reading are also features of a Taizé service and, along with the music, often flow from one to another accompanied by periods of silence for reflection.

Parishes large and small throughout the world incorporate Taizé chants within their worship life. One of the most famous churches to adopt this model is All Saints' Episcopal Church in Beverly Hills, California, where Taizé services were pioneered by director of music Thomas Foster over his long tenure from 1976 to 2003.[21] Whether individual chants are included in traditional eucharistic or daily prayer liturgies or worship is designed to more fully focus on the music and format of a Taizé service, the spirit of Brother Roger and his philosophical emphasis on ecumenism and an inclusive spirit make the Taizé chants appropriate in a variety of settings, and the music and liturgical format of the worship of the Taizé community are being incorporated by many denominations.

JAZZ
Jazz is a distinctly American musical idiom that combines elements of African rhythm and European harmony with roots in spirituals, working songs, and field hollers of former African-American slaves. Blues is the most significant forerunner of jazz and forms the basis of the genre's earliest experiments. Like European classical music, jazz went through many variations and styles over the course of its comparatively short history, including ragtime, classic "New Orleans" jazz, hot jazz, swing, bebop, cool, hard bop, bossa nova, modal, and free jazz. Contemporary jazz since 1970 has consisted of many different types of fusion genres in addition to the blues. Improvisation is an essential element of jazz; virtually all jazz performers improvise regularly regardless of the specific jazz style they are performing.

It may seem ironic that a secular style that had its roots in dance halls and red-light districts would find its way into liturgical worship, but that is precisely what is happening in some Episcopal parishes throughout the United States. While not altogether common, some churches have even begun regular "jazz masses." Canterbury House, the Episcopal student ministry of the University of Michigan, has earned a national reputation for their jazz masses, which have become highly successful over the past several decades. Jazz and jazz-related styles permeate every aspect of Canterbury House's worship services. The eucharistic liturgy is still followed, but alternative musical styles are explored. Psalms, for instance, have formulas that seem to resemble Anglican chant, but upon closer inspection are revealed to be jazz progressions. Canterbury House also explores variety in their congregational singing styles, exploring Southern Harmony and Gospel singing in addition to traditional hymn singing. The result has been a highly dynamic worship style that has created a vibrant liturgical experience for young people at the University of Michigan.[22]

While Canterbury House's services have been pioneering in many ways, jazz, spirituality, and religion have been mingling with each other for decades. High-profile examples within the jazz industry include Louis Armstrong's *Louis and the Good Book* (1958), John Coltrane's *A Love Supreme* (1965), Duke Ellington's three sacred concerts (1965, 1968, and 1973), and Dave Brubeck's *To Hope! A Celebration* (1996). Some churches began experimenting with jazz styles as early as the 1960s. Father John Garcia Gensel established a "ministry to the jazz community" at St. Peter's Church in New York City in 1965. A quotation from Father Gensel serves as an appropriate conclusion to this section:

> I've learned that there is a *depth to jazz* that parallels scripture. Jazz is a music that is harmonically rich. Jazz melodies are intricate and take unexpected twists and turns. Jazz rhythms are vibrant and complex. Jazz honors diversity. Jazz requires

a lifelong pursuit of understanding—there is always more to learn/discover. Yet there is something in jazz that touches and speaks to people.[23]

THE IONA COMMUNITY

The Iona Community was founded in Glasgow and Iona, Scotland, in 1938 by George MacLeod. Members of the community rebuilt and lived within the monastic quarters of a medieval abbey, where they established their principles of hospitality, inclusion, spirituality, social justice, human rights, environmental stewardship, peacemaking, non-violence, healing, and reconciliation. Iona remains a center for tourism, hosting daily worship for anyone who makes the pilgrimage.

The Iona Community has fostered its own musical traditions as well. John Bell, its most influential writer and composer of hymns, has published many collections of worship resources, songs, and psalm tunes through the Wild Goose Resource Group, the official publishing arm of the Iona Community (and available in the United States through GIA). The emphasis in all of these publications is spiritual community building through congregational song. Bell has also offered several books on the importance of congregational singing, and frequently travels as a clinician, giving workshops on congregational song as practiced by the Iona Community.

Like the music of Taizé, the songs of Iona are often short, repetitive chants, easily sung and harmonized without the aid of words or music on paper. While Taizé chants are designed to encourage prayer and meditation, the texts of the Iona Community echo Iona's commitment to issues of social justice and faith. Worship in the Iona tradition may include full liturgies written by members of the community or simply the incorporation of Iona-related songs and chants into a parish's musical repertoire.

PAPERLESS MUSIC
(MUSIC THAT MAKES COMMUNITY)

Closely related to the Taizé and Iona communities' ideal of congregational music making is the recent American movement incorporating "paperless" music into worship. The concept of paperless music is based on folk traditions and building community through singing music that has been learned "by heart," free from traditional score-based notation systems. In his introduction to *Music by Heart*, a collection of eighty-five paperless songs, Donald Schell writes:

> What does singing "by heart" mean to you? To me it immediately suggests singing something known by memory and loved. It's also a feeling. Songs we know by heart come to us in a distinct, recognizable way, their words and music seemingly flowing out of us, continuous, effortless, and whole. A crowd (church or secular) singing "Amazing Grace" knows where they're going. You can feel the music has come to mean more than the words, and that the moment connects to something more universal. And when it's by heart there's also something fresh and new in the moment, though the song is familiar. The music we sing by heart we've learned whole. Our memory connects mind, heartbeat and breath. It makes us feel whole.[24]

Over the past decade, paperless music-making has been encouraged by an organization called Music That Makes Community, which has developed a series of workshops designed to promote congregational singing within church communities. Music That Makes Community was founded by Donald Schell, Rick Fabian, and Emily Scott as an extension of Donald and Rick's liturgical work at St. Gregory of Nyssa Episcopal Church in San Francisco, California. Collectively, they had "a desire to have music for worship that would leave congregants free to move around, use their hands, and be fully present to one another in worship."[25] The theological spirit at the heart of their ministry is deep and inclusive:

This work is essentially a practice of hospitality that welcomes all into a group collaborating in making music.... We seek to engage our whole mental, physical and spiritual attention in worship. Our fully engaged presence is our best gift to one another and to God. In order to connect in a real, honest way, we must be vulnerable to one another. We take risks in our leadership, and when we choose the wrong pitch or our voices crack or a song doesn't work, we model forgiveness. We live into the dissonance and consider it all part of the holy work of coming together in song, in worship, in our life as the body of Christ.[26]

Although a recent phenomenon, the popularity of paperless music is rapidly spreading throughout the Episcopal Church. As of 2014, over 650 musicians, pastors, and lay parishioners have been trained by official Music That Makes Community workshops.

SOUTHERN UNITED STATES AND AFRICAN-AMERICAN TRADITIONS

Closely related to jazz are several other distinctly American musical styles, including Southern harmony or shape-note singing, African-American spirituals, and gospel. Each of these styles has been explored within Episcopal worship to various degrees over the past several decades.

Southern Harmony refers to a style of hymn singing that developed in the southern United States in the eighteenth and nineteenth centuries. The name derives from one of two major collections of these hymns: *The Southern Harmony and Musical Companion* (1835) by William Walker and *The Sacred Harp* (1844) by Benjamin Franklin White and Elisha James King. Both of these collections employed "shape note" singing. Shape note music, as the name implies, uses different shapes for each note in the musical scale as a pedagogical tool to increase sight-reading facility. Sacred Harp songs are generally performed unaccompanied. Most of the texts are scripture-oriented, and Sacred Harp singing occurs either at Sunday morning worship services or community social gatherings. Although shape note singing is not practiced within the Episcopal Church, hymns from these two major collections are still a part of the repertoire. Specific examples from *The Hymnal 1982* include "Brightest and Best of the Stars of the Morning" (STAR IN THE EAST, 118), "Come Away to the Skies" (MIDDLEBURY, 213), "What Wondrous Love Is This" (WONDROUS LOVE, 439), and "How Firm a Foundation" (FOUNDATION, 636).

Spirituals are African-American religious folk songs that date from the eighteenth and nineteenth centuries. During the nineteenth and early twentieth centuries they were collected and introduced to the public at large by well-known composers and arrangers. Many of these tunes are easily recognizable, and some appear as hymns in *The Hymnal 1982*. By including WERE YOU THERE (as Hymn 80), *The Hymnal 1940* was the first mainline hymnal to incorporate a distinctly African-American piece of music, and *The Hymnal 1982* includes eight hymns from African-American culture.

Stylistically, spirituals often employ a call-and-response format and refrains. Themes depict the struggles of a hard life combined with deep faith and a sense of determined optimism. Famous composers and arrangers of spirituals include Harry T. Burleigh, R. Nathaniel Dett, Hall Johnson, William Dawson, Jester Hairston, Horace Clarence Boyer, and Moses Hogan. Early versions of spirituals were also archived by nineteenth-century collectors in shape note publications.

Gospel is a distinctly African-American style of sacred music, closely related to blues and the spiritual. Originally written for and still used in worship, it includes both choral and solo pieces, with Mahalia Jackson as its most famous exponent. Gospel music features simple melodies that are embellished through improvisation.

PRAISE MUSIC

Praise music is usually rock- or pop-influenced tunes with Christian lyrics used during worship in many circles of evangelical Christianity. Praise music should not be confused with "contemporary Christian music," which refers to the Christian music industry as a whole and which thrives upon airplay, concerts, and recordings. Although this latter term is sometimes used as a synonym with praise music, contemporary Christian music is a broad label that includes pop artists who sing Christian lyrics but do not necessarily work for a church or use their music in a liturgical context. It usually refers to the industry and the genre, whereas "praise music" refers to music that is actually used in worship. The two flavors of the genre draw from largely the same repertoire of songs and conventions.

While praise music is ubiquitous within evangelical circles of Christianity, the genre has made comparatively little impact within the Episcopal Church compared to other mainline denominations. Time will be the ultimate judge as to whether praise music finds a larger place within the Episcopal Church.

EMERGENT MUSIC (ECUMENICAL TRADITIONS)

Over the past two decades, a new form of worship has begun to take shape within the movement called the "emerging church." Fiercely ecumenical in nature, participants describe themselves as Protestant, post-Protestant, evangelical, post-evangelical, liberal, post-liberal, conservative, post-conservative, anabaptist, adventist, reformed, charismatic, neo-charismatic, and post-charismatic. Emerging churches are spreading rapidly, with establishments in North America, Europe, Africa, and Australia. Emergent Christians seek to connect with ancient traditions as they have one eye fixed firmly on the future.

As emerging communities are both newly formed and (by their very nature) not denominational, there is no cohesive musical tradition within the emergent church. Rather, these

worshippers draw upon a wide variety of resources. Isaac
Everett, in the introduction to his book *The Emergent Psalter,*
observes that "with a few exceptions, the emerging church has
yet to create a musical identity for itself," though it has sparked
a resurgence of interest in ancient forms of liturgy and spiritual
practice:

> This return to ancient practice does not necessarily coincide
> with a return to theological orthodoxy. In fact, emerging
> Christians are discovering that the mystery and ambiguity of
> ritual meshes with a postmodern worldview in a way that
> their past experiences of worship haven't. This renewal of tra-
> dition doesn't signify a renewed commitment to religious in-
> stitutions, either, which are often mistrusted by emerging
> Christians. Rather than adopt a single liturgical traditional
> wholesale, emerging Christians are drawing from a variety of
> traditions to create a personalized, à la carte spiritual practice,
> and I've seen emergent communities rediscovering everything
> from incense to altar calls. One common thread, however, is
> an emphasis on practices that "integrate body and spirit," fo-
> cusing on actions rather than words, which engage an entire
> community in collaborative, interactive worship.[27]

Everett, a composer, goes on to discuss the process of cap-
turing the essence of ancient texts through a contemporary
musical language that draws upon a wide variety of sources.
His *magnum opus* is an "emergent psalter," which explores new
ways of singing and playing the psalms without the aid of an
organ or four-part choir. Everett's approach offers a glimpse
of what liturgical worship and church music itself might look
like in a postmodern, emergent age.

Q QUESTIONS FOR REFLECTION AND DISCUSSION

1. Like *The Hymnal 1982,* Taizé, Iona, and paperless traditions emphasize congregational participation above all. Has your church made use of any of these resources? Do you think these styles would be successful vehicles for enhancing corporate worship within your parish?

2. Unlike plainchant and hymnody, some contemporary worship styles have their roots in secular music. Jazz, rock, and rap styles, for example, originally contained lyrics that emphasized romantic liaisons, sensuality, sexuality, and secular social issues. Is it an unusual experience for you to hear these styles with sacred lyrics in a liturgical context? Are you able to successfully separate the music from its original sociological context? Why or why not?

3. Over the next month, explore the styles mentioned in this chapter through CDs, MP3 downloads, or YouTube videos. What styles are most appealing to you? Do you feel that your spiritual experience could be enriched through the exploration of these alternative musical traditions?

The Future of Music in the Episcopal Church

It's structured like any other Episcopal Eucharist and begins in the same manner—with one difference: it has a beat you can (and are encouraged to) dance to. In place of a choir there's likely a small table with two turntables set up side by side and a DJ, head bobbing to the prelude, with a hand on each, either syncing up the next beat, or putting the current track together. In a larger service there may be a full band providing the music, while in a smaller service as little as a powerful portable boom box may be doing the job. Leading the music, coming in generally when a choir would (and otherwise shouting encouragement when a choir would, likely, not) are a coterie of rappers.... The music is loud and exuberant. The rappers call out "God is in the House!"

Lucas Smith, "The HipHopEMass" [28]

The liturgy is the "HipHopEMass" which has been developed at Trinity Episcopal Church in Morrisania in the Bronx, New York City. To the traditional Episcopalian, such a service may seem foreign or shocking. However, the Episcopal Church has always been an institution of change, and liturgies are contin-

uing to change as the decades move forward. Social and theological shifts are often followed by musical ones: the revision
of the Book of Common Prayer in 1979, for example, resulted
in a more diverse and eclectic hymnal a few years later.

I completed this manuscript during the summer of 2014,
at the same time that the Episcopal Church celebrated the fortieth anniversary of the Philadelphia Eleven—the first group
of women ordained as priests in the Episcopal Church on July
29, 1974. In 2006, just thirty-two years later, Katharine Jef-
ferts Schori was elected the first female Presiding Bishop of
the Episcopal Church. In 2004, Gene Robinson was installed
amidst controversy as the first openly gay bishop in the Episcopal Church. In 2012, just eight years later, the Episcopal
Church authorized for trial use "The Witnessing and Blessing
of a Lifelong Covenant" for same-gender couples. What is at
first radical becomes not only accepted, but celebrated as time
passes. Will the next revision of the Episcopal hymnal include
a hip-hop selection?

One can often predict the future by studying the past. If
this is true, music in the Episcopal Church will continue to
include a unique blend of tradition and innovation within a
strong liturgical framework. It is likely that Anglican chant
and classic anthems will still be sung one hundred years from
now. But it is equally likely that newer styles will merge with
traditional ones to form creative new liturgies that we cannot
yet imagine. Ultimately, sacred music is not measured by its
form or style, but by its effectiveness: music enhances worship,
elevates texts, moves people to deep spiritual places, and
evokes the spirit and power of God.

Notes

1. Oliver Sacks, *Musicophilia: Tales of Music and the Brain* (New York: Alfred A. Knopf, 2007), xi.

2. Canon 24, Section 1, reprinted in the frontmatter of *The Hymnal 1982*.

3. This topic is beyond the scope of this particular book, but is covered extensively in Vicki K. Black's *Welcome to the Church Year: An Introduction to the Seasons of the Episcopal Church* (Harrisburg: Morehouse Publishing, 2004).

4. Raymond F. Glover, "What Is Congregational Song?," *The Hymnal 1982 Companion*, Volume I, ed. Raymond F. Glover (New York: Church Hymnal Corporation, 1990), 4.

5. Glover, "What Is Congregational Song?", 5–6.

6. Preface to *The Hymnal 1940*, iii.

7. Leonard L. Ellinwood and Charles G. Manns, "The Publication of the Hymnal of the Episcopal Church," in Glover, ed., *The Hymnal 1982 Companion*, Volume I, 75.

8. Preface to *The Hymnal 1982*.

9. Preface to *Wonder, Love, and Praise* (New York: Church Publishing, 1997).

10. Preface to *Wonder, Love, and Praise*.

11. Preface to *Voices Found: Women in the Church's Song* (New York: Church Publishing, 2003).

12. "The Hymnal Revision Feasibility Study: A Report to the Standing Commission on Liturgy and Music" (New York: Church Pension Group Office of Research, 2011), 66.

13. The Book of Common Prayer suggests specific hymns on only three occasions: Palm Sunday, Good Friday, and at ordinations.

14. For example, when the minor tune LLANGLOFFAN (Hymns 68 and 607 in *The Hymnal 1982*) is changed to a major key, the tune name becomes LLANFYLLIN (Hymn 570, first tune, in *The Hymnal 1940*).

15. Don Michael Randel, ed., *The New Harvard Dictionary of Music* (Cambridge, Mass.: Belknap Press of Harvard University Press, 1986), 667.

16. Christopher Hill, Preface to *The New St Paul's Cathedral Psalter*, ed. John Scott (Norwich: Canterbury Press, 1997), viii.

17. Alec Wyton, ed., *The Anglican Chant Psalter* (New York: Church Publishing, 1987), 12.

18. Additional canticles and daily office liturgies can be found in *Enriching Our Worship: Morning and Evening Prayer, the Great Litany, the Holy Eucharist* (New York: Church Publishing, 1998).

19. For more information about national organ traditions, please consult *The Cambridge Companion to the Organ,* ed. Nicholas Thistlethwaite and Geoffrey Webber (New York: Cambridge University Press, 1999).

20. "The Hymnal Revision Feasibility Study," 39.

21. See Thomas Foster, "Taizé at All Saints' Episcopal Church, Beverly Hills, California," in *What Would Jesus Sing?: Experimentation and Tradition in Church Music,* ed. Marilyn L. Haskel (New York: Church Publishing, 2007).

22. See Reid Hamilton and Stephen Rush, *Better Get It in Your Soul: What Liturgists Can Learn from Jazz* (New York: Church Publishing, 2008).

23. Richard Birk, "What About Jazz?," in Haskel, ed., *What Would Jesus Sing?, 8.*

24. Donald Schell, "Singing from the Heart," in All Saints Company, *Music by Heart: Paperless Songs for Evening Worship* (New York: Church Publishing, 2008), 1.

25. www.musicthatmakescommunity.org/history.

26. www.musicthatmakescommunity.org/core_values.

27. Isaac Everett, *The Emergent Psalter* (New York: Church Publishing, 2009), 1–2.

28. Lucas Smith, "The HipHopEMass," in Haskel, ed., *What Would Jesus Sing?, 181.*

Suggestions for Further Reading

LITURGICAL RESOURCES

The Book of Common Prayer. New York: Church Hymnal Corporation, 1979.

Enriching Our Worship: Morning and Evening Prayer, The Great Litany, The Holy Eucharist. New York: Church Publishing, 1998.

An Episcopal Dictionary of the Church: A User-Friendly Reference for Episcopalians. By Donald S. Armentrout and Robert Boak Slocum. New York: Church Publishing, 2000.

The Hymnal 1982 Companion. Edited by Raymond F. Glover. 4 volumes. New York: Church Hymnal Corporation, 1990–1994.

Liturgical Music for the Revised Common Lectionary. Three Volumes: Years A, B, and C. Edited by Thomas Pavlechko and Carl P. Daw, Jr. New York: Church Publishing, 2007–2009.

Lord, Open Our Lips: Musical Help for Leaders of the Liturgy. New York: Church Publishing, 2000.

HYMNALS

El Himnario. New York: Church Publishing, 1998.

The Hymnal 1940. New York: Church Pension Fund, 1940.

The Hymnal 1982. New York: Church Publishing, 1985.

Lift Every Voice and Sing II: An African American Hymnal. New York: Church Publishing, 1993.

Music by Heart: Paperless Songs for Evening Worship. New York: Church Publishing, 2008.

My Heart Sings Out. Edited by Fiona Vidal-White. New York: Church Publishing, 2005.

Voices Found: Women in the Church's Song. New York: Church Publishing, 2003.

Wonder, Love, and Praise: A Supplement to The Hymnal 1982. New York: Church Publishing, 1997.

PSALTERS AND PSALMODY

The Anglican Chant Psalter. Edited by Alec Wyton. New York: Church Hymnal Corporation, 1987.

Countryman, L. William. *Conversations with Scriptures: The Psalms.* Harrisburg: Morehouse Publishing, 2013.

Crafton, Barbara Cawthorne. *Meditations on the Psalms for Every Day of the Year.* Harrisburg: Morehouse Publishing, 2003.

Gradual Psalms with Alleluia Verses and Tracts: Years A, B, and C for the Revised Common Lectionary. New York: Church Publishing, 2007.

A HymnTune Psalter. Two Volumes. Edited by Carl P. Daw, Jr., and Kevin R. Hackett. New York: Church Publishing, 2007, 2008.

The Saint Helena Psalter: A New Version of the Psalms in Expansive Language. Edited by the Order of St. Helena. New York: Church Publishing, 2000.

The New St Paul's Cathedral Psalter. Edited by John Scott. Norwich: Canterbury Press, 1997.

CHURCH HISTORY

MacCulloch, Diarmaid. *Christianity: The First Three Thousand Years.* New York: Penguin Books, 2009.

Prichard, Robert W. *A History of the Episcopal Church.* Third revised edition. Harrisburg: Morehouse Publishing, 2014.

EPISCOPAL CHURCH MUSIC

Everett, Isaac. *The Emergent Psalter.* New York: Church Publishing, 2009.

Hamilton, Reid, and Stephen Rush. *Better Get It in Your Soul: What Liturgists Can Learn from Jazz.* New York: Church Publishing, 2008.

Haskel, Marilyn L., ed. *What Would Jesus Sing? Experimentation and Tradition in Church Music.* New York: Church Publishing, 2007.

Hatchett, Marion J. *A Manual for Clergy and Church Musicians.* New York: Church Hymnal Corporation, 1980.

Rideout, Marti. *All Things Necessary: A Practical Guide for Episcopal Church Musicians.* New York: Church Publishing, 2012.

Roth, Nancy. *A Closer Walk: Meditating on Hymns for Year A.* New York: Church Publishing, 1998.

———. *Awake, My Soul!: Meditating on Hymns for Year B.* New York: Church Publishing, 1999.

———. *New Every Morning: Meditating on Hymns for Year C.* New York: Church Publishing, 2000.

Routley, Erik, and Lionel Dakers. *A Short History of English Church Music.* Second Edition. New York: Continuum Books, 1997.

Sirota, Victoria. *Preaching to the Choir: Claiming the Role of the Sacred Musician.* New York: Church Publishing, 2006.

WELCOME TO SERIES

Black, Vicki K. *Welcome to Anglican Spiritual Traditions.* Harrisburg: Morehouse Publishing, 2011.

———. *Welcome to the Book of Common Prayer.* Harrisburg: Morehouse Publishing, 2005.

———. *Welcome to the Church Year: An Introduction to the Seasons of the Episcopal Church.* Harrisburg: Morehouse Publishing, 2004.

Black, Vicki K., and Peter Wenner. *Welcome to the Bible.* Harrisburg: Morehouse Publishing, 2007.

Webber, Christopher L. *Welcome to the Christian Faith.* Harrisburg: Morehouse Publishing, 2011.

———. *Welcome to the Episcopal Church: An Introduction to Its History, Faith, and Worship.* Harrisburg: Morehouse Publishing, 1999.

———. *Welcome to Sunday: An Introduction to Worship in the Episcopal Church.* Harrisburg: Morehouse Publishing, 2003.

Listening to Church Music

There is a famous phrase—sometimes attributed to actor Martin Mull—that states "writing about music is like dancing about architecture." The point is well taken. The music described in this book ultimately has to be experienced by the reader.

To listen to the anthems, psalms, and hymns of the traditional Anglican canon, one of the best places to start is a series of CDs produced by Sir John Scott and the St. Paul's Cathedral Choir, all released by Hyperion Records in London: *The English Anthem* (8 volumes); *The English Hymn* (5 volumes); and *The Psalms of David* (12 volumes). The latter volume is a particularly impressive collection, gathering together recordings of all 150 Psalms sung to Anglican chant. *The English Anthem Collection: 1540–1988* (4 CDs, Alto Records) by John Harper and the Magdalen College Choir, Oxford, also offers a generous sampling of anthems. *The Treasury of English Church Music: 1100–1965* (5 CDs, EMI records) offers an historical survey of English music from the medieval era to the twentieth century. Extensive liner notes are included.

Priory Records (UK) is also devoted exclusively to recording and releasing church music. Notable collections released under this label include *Great Cathedral Anthems* (12 volumes), *Magnificat and Nunc Dimittis* (21 volumes), *The New*

English Hymnal (23 volumes), *The Psalms of David* (10 volumes), and *Te Deum and Jubilate* (4 volumes).

The Choir of Guilford Cathedral, conducted by Barry Rose, has released recordings of Stainer's *Crucifixion* and Maunder's *Olivet to Calvary.* Both works have been released as a two CD-set on the EMI label. In addition, King's College, Cambridge has released several famous recordings of its annual Festival of Nine Lessons and Carols. All are recommended.

Organ recordings are manifold. A good place to start is the collection *Great Cathedral Organs* (13 CDs, EMI).

Church Publishing, Inc. offers numerous CDs from American Episcopal choirs, including some devoted to more contemporary worship styles. Many larger Episcopal cathedrals and churches also produce their own discographies.

www.ingramcontent.com/pod-product-compliance
Lightning Source LLC
Jackson TN
JSHW011403130125
77033JS00023B/816